PENGUIN BOOKS
THE MAN WHO WOULD BE QUEEN

Hoshang Merchant inherits his moralism from his Zoroastrian grandfathers, his aestheticism from a neurotic mother and his hedonism from his father—a young widow's heir. Trained in the West, Merchant chose to study Eastern religions during his travels; a democrat by education, he is aristocratic by instinct; an intuitive poet, he is a professor by profession. He has published many collections of poetry and is the editor of *Yaarana: Gay Writing from South Asia*. He lives alone in Hyderabad in a home he has made for himself where he fathers his books, his students and a young friend.

The Man Who Would Be Queen
Autobiographical Fictions

HOSHANG MERCHANT

PENGUIN BOOKS

PENGUIN BOOKS

Published by the Penguin Group

Penguin Books India Pvt. Ltd, 11 Community Centre, Panchsheel Park, New Delhi 110 017, India

Penguin Group (USA) Inc., 375 Hudson Street, New York, New York 10014, USA

Penguin Group (Canada), 90 Eglinton Avenue East, Suite 700, Toronto, Ontario, M4P 2Y3, Canada (a division of Pearson Penguin Canada Inc.)

Penguin Books Ltd, 80 Strand, London WC2R 0RL, England

Penguin Ireland, 25 St Stephen's Green, Dublin 2, Ireland (a division of Penguin Books Ltd)

Penguin Group (Australia), 250 Camberwell Road, Camberwell, Victoria 3124, Australia (a division of Pearson Australia Group Pty Ltd)

Penguin Group (NZ), 67 Apollo Drive, Rosedale, Auckland 0632, New Zealand

Penguin Group (South Africa) (Pty) Ltd, 24 Sturdee Avenue, Rosebank, Johannesburg 2196, South Africa

Penguin Books Ltd, Registered Offices: 80 Strand, London WC2R 0RL, England

First published by Penguin Books India 2011

Copyright © Hoshang Merchant 2011

All rights reserved

10 9 8 7 6 5 4 3 2 1

The views and opinions expressed in this book are the author's own and the facts are as reported by him which have been verified to the extent possible, and the publishers are not in any way liable for the same.

ISBN 9780143064862

Typeset in DanteMT by R. Ajith Kumar, New Delhi
Printed at Manipal Technology Limited, Manipal

This book is sold subject to the condition that it shall not, by way of trade or otherwise, be lent, resold, hired out, or otherwise circulated without the publisher's prior written consent in any form of binding or cover other than that in which it is published and without a similar condition including this condition being imposed on the subsequent purchaser and without limiting the rights under copyright reserved above, no part of this publication may be reproduced, stored in or introduced into a retrieval system, or transmitted in any form or by any means (electronic, mechanical, photocopying, recording or otherwise), without the prior written permission of both the copyright owner and the above-mentioned publisher of this book.

Contents

THE GARDEN OF DELIGHT	1
No Man's Land	3
The Dead Sea	20
The Sea of Fertility	40
CIRCLE OF HELL	103
Nablus	106
Jerusalem (1983–84)	127
GARDEN OF BLISS	151
Why I Write	154
How I Write	163
I AM NOT IN	173

Garden of Delight

I
No Man's Land

Youth: India, 1947–1968
We are all murderers and prostitutes—no matter to what culture, society, class, nation one belongs, no matter how normal, moral or mature, one takes oneself to be.

—R.D. Laing
Politics of Experience

These two then (which Avicen calleth the Corascene bitch and the Armenian dogge)... being put together in the vessel of the sepulcher, doe bit one another cruelly, and by their great poyson and furious rage, they never leave one another... till both of them by their slavering venom and mortall hurts, be all of a goarebloud, over all the parts of their bodies; and finally killing one another after their death, changeth before which time, they loose in their corruption and putrification, their first natural formes, to take afterwards one onely new, more noble, and better forme.

—An Alchemic Text

> Do you wish to go naked before your friend?... He who makes no secret of himself excites anger in others: That is how much reason you have to fear nakedness! If you were gods you could then be ashamed of your clothes!
>
> —Nietzsche
> *Thus Spoke Zarathustra*

My first impression of my mother is her moving around my sickroom. Her hair was down to her waist. She wore a green kimono.

My first photo shows me seated in the lap of 'granny,' an elderly neighbour. I am frowning, my hands cup my face. The yellow print dress was my favourite. (My grandparents disapproved of my parents' marriage since mother was a divorcee.) Father took the photograph in the late afternoon sun. I sat in grandfather's lap and pulled his beard. Once I wore his priest's cap as he napped.

The barred window is still there to which I clung before being sent off to school. I would sit in class with elder sister. Father was remote: a young face in dark glasses looking over my crib during malaria fevers. I had 'incurable' eczema. At birth I bled hours from the severed umbilicus. Once an insect bite on the penis: mother beat a 'confession' out of me, father carried me to a doctor. During haircuts I wept and was given caraway seed-candies. I hated boarding school and was brought home in days.

Arrival of a new baby: father placed collyrium, rose water, rice, a silver rupee, a vigil lamp, a portrait of Zoroaster, pen, ink and paper in a 'puja' tray. The goddess of good fortune would write the newborn's future. I would sit in my sister's crib and feed her milk out of a bottle. Mother lay in a hospital room amid a scent of phlox. As we left her with the tiny new baby she pined.

I was the only boy at school. Mother had decided I wouldn't swear or be rough. I sang, danced, cooked and sewed. I could not thread needles. I hated English but loved history. At home I dressed in a sari and sang and danced under the cherry tree with sister. My parents did not like this. One day a man came with a tin box strapped to his neck. Atop the box was a rag doll whose hands he manipulated with a string tied to his toe. For an anna each, children could press an eye to one of the two windows of this magic box and see views:

Delhi ka Durbar dekho
Agra ka Taj Mahal dekho
Kathputli ka nautch dekho
Vyjanthimala dekho
Dekho bacche dekho

Only his commentary did not have anything to do with the images in the magic lantern.

At seven I became a Zoroastrian. My grandfather, an aunt of mother's (her mother died insane), god's 101 names. I addressed fervent prayers to a rosy-cheeked man whose blond locks coiled around him like snakes. His turban was like grandfather's. I went to school, returned and after dinner prayed and fell asleep instantly. In Zoroaster's huge fire temple portrait I saw only his feet. I wore a sacred girdle round my waist, 'to separate the lofty from the gross.'

We moved from our two-room apartment to a vast bungalow by the sea, with a fernery and a wild bamboo garden. The house was green and built athwart a hill. At ebb tide I saw rocks come up from the water. I dreamed of lost continents. It rained days. The brain-fever bird. Jasmine. The old chandelier dropped crystals we collected.

Dropping us off at school each morning father tarried at the shopping centre exchanging compliments with the pharmacist, the laundry girls, the storekeepers. He was known by his six-cylinder Morris with a Great Britain license plate. Doors were opened for him as he arrived late for work, at his traditional hour. As he went through the mills' printing, sizing or dyeing departments he hauled up idling workers, his fits of temper and abuses ringing from the tin-roofs. Then he was served breakfast: eggs in butter, without peppers. Lunch from the mess was rounded off by a nap in a low chair. A masseur suspended him six inches from the earth daily. He walked better when let down again.

Then a shower in the specially installed shower stall and fresh hankies and cologne to beat the heat. Then holding of court for labour problems with slaps meted out to offenders. Then came flowers from the company gardens: carnations, cannas, roses, which mother arranged for evening tea. But father had come up the hard way. After repudiating an inheritance he started off again washing dyestuff drums for Rs 75 a month. Now he received pay-offs from dyestuff dealers for business favours.

During summer vacations in Poona we saw the ex-Maharani Chimnabai Gaekwar of Baroda drive by on the Bund in a '30s Rolls-Royce. She wore chiffon and pearls and, as the car rolled by at 5 mph, we saw the old face impassive and white, laced with wrinkles. Her equally impassive Indian chauffeur tooled her home around sunset. Mother told us she had poisoned the Gaekwar's heir to further the chances of her own son.

On a visit to an old palace we saw the royal bed, where a dog had littered.

My parents quarrelled. A policeman stationed to ward off bootleggers often intervened. Grandfather sided with father, menfolk with menfolk.

A court-clerk arrived with a paper for my mother to sign. She wept. Father wasn't home. He'd sued for divorce. Eden fled. We were herded in the six-cylinder Morris and taken to a lawyer. Could we choose between our parents? Our parents reconciled. Mother bought an emerald and crystal for her roses, father, a gramophone and waltzes.

I went to a boys' school. I didn't play cricket. The lady teacher liked me, so did the Jesuit. A phone call for me: 'Why did you volunteer to go to a boarding school?' Father had sued for divorce a second time. That recess I was particularly alone. When father came to fetch me for boarding school I refused to go. I started taking the suburban train 14 kms to school. I recited a prepared speech before a judge: 'If I'm separated from mother, I'd die.'
My parents were reconciled again. I saw them kissing. He was in trouble at work.

On a train a stranger 'protected' me in the rush. He didn't let go of me even when crowds lessened. I didn't believe my friend who told me the stranger's intent.
A group of boys gathered around a *Playboy* centrefold of a nude in a red veil. I was uninterested. The big boy of our class displayed his member. The Jesuit broke up our gathering. I confessed to mother. I had wet dreams. I learnt the word 'overflow'. Mother was disbelieving.

Every Saturday afternoon father took me out to lunch: fruit salad, and ice cream. A girl joined us. I liked her as I was always alone. Aunts, uncles, cousins, grandparents I knew none, nor playmates. Mother questioned me: Was she young? Was she fair? I fabulated, played to my mother's worst expectations of the girl, pitiful and indignant that mother should have a rival. We never saw the girl again.

At school I was shy. I hated mathematics. I liked memory-drawing. The art master touched me once but I moved away. I took up dramatics. All the female roles came to me: Martha in a Christmas pageant, the mother in Amahl and the Night-visitors, the wife in These Cornfields, played as if she were Lady Macbeth in a veil since wigs and falsies were taboo. I won a prize for my portrayal of a hen pecked husband. I had a beard coming.

Mother was arthritic. Now she was crippled and walked with crutches. At the nursing home a rat gnawed at her in her sleep. She could not afford another place. Father had left yet again: Case no. 36 of 163. Things were beyond me.
   Mother was locked out of the house. She cut her arm on the glass door. She defended herself and struck father on the forehead with a stone. For the first time I saw father weep. A servant attended to him. The servant restrained my mother from going to the sea to drown herself. There was a curse on my mother, doomed to lamentation on each auspicious occasion. Dinners were thrown on the floor. We were startled out of bed, lights went up, mother screamed all night for help from neighbours. I went to the police with

my mother in nightclothes. I did not know why my parents married, nor did the school psychiatrist who asked me to be a curator.

Younger sister and I drew blood from each other. I decided not to be a surgeon when my own blood sickened me. As children, elder sister and I had excluded younger sister from 'Heaven': though beautiful and lucky she was 'tainted', we said.

Elder sister and I decided to play 'house'. We partitioned the house and posted a sign 'Hippo, stay out' to antagonize mother, who peered through the ventilators now and then. We went out on food 'raids'. Our house within a house did not last long. Father accused me of sleeping with sister.

My effeminacy antagonized father. During their fights I stood square between mother and him. Disturbed by this sign of maleness he aimed at my genitals.

It was I who touched the man on the suburban train. He came in his trousers. He took me to a carpenter's attic. Amid sawdust he penetrated me. I felt pain and loss. He offered me a candy.

Picking up a man for Saturday afternoons: I would be at the railway station at eight each morning at the foot of the bridge to see men descending.. I would first see feet, then groin, torso, face in that order.

A stray lock, a weak eye, flared nostrils, a paunch—

something would have to be attractive. I would follow him into the overcrowded compartment. After the initial accidental strokes and brushes I would have his genitals in my hands. This done wordlessly for days each morning, finally I would be invited home. Sometimes, from an evening train home, we would end up on the beach. I thought I was cursed with an orgasmless life. I looked up 'homosexual' in the dictionary. I didn't sleep with the same man twice for fear of scandal. But my secret was out. I confessed to sister, who told mother, who complained to father, who wept by the sea, sent me to a therapist and asked me to be a man.

Then he tried tenderness with me. I had fallen in love with a classmate in my last year of school. I kept chaste for him, started an adolescent diary, dreamed of running away with him and living with him forever. It did not happen. I tried suicide, pills. Nothing happened. Father, tired and remorseful, asked if we hadn't heard of the 'Chinvat' bridge in the Zoroastrian heaven that suicides can never cross. Daena (conscience), for that was also mother's name, would meet me and say, 'I am ugly for your action has made me so.' She was to be a fair maiden.

My college friend fell in love with sister. From her I learnt how to pine, quarrel, show mock anger, lure and finally attain. The boy's father ran a Ferris wheel at the fiesta of Mary of the Mount. Each September we would climb to Mary's church with mother, past shops selling votive limbs, legs, arms, even babies, in wax to be offered at the altar. Mary was said to have come out of the sea. She trod on a serpent or on a moon-crescent. Ave Maria. Mother's birthday fell then: first of the five ritual days for the dead, preceding the Zoroastrian harvest rites. Mother on losing a child had been promised many more by Mary in a dream. Now mother was legless, father was gone. We were alone. I lost god.

Father brought us Advice to Adolescents: 'Do not masturbate dear children, it will blind you.'

'There is a river whose water may never fall on earth, a tree whose roots are above and whose fruits are to be reverted before they fall.'

The untouchable people had washed toilets for generations. She was customarily let in through a window on which rested a small wooden ladder. Mother was the first one to let her come in to work through the front door. Now and then she chatted about her family with mother, squatting on the floor and sipping tea from a broken china cup set aside for her. Like everyone in Bombay she wanted to get rich quick in the film industry. Her favourite fantasy role was that of a drunk—she probably ran a still in her shantytown hut. Her wealth she wore: two gold earrings so heavy that they had torn the earlobes.

The other servant was a Brahmin from North India. He wore a pigtail and the sacred thread—his caste marks. Though a vegetarian he helped out with the cooking of meat at home. He was a mill labourer brought home by father. Mother suspected him of being a spy; that he was mercenary there's no doubt. But when he filled the water pots towards evening he sang loudly from the Tulsi *Ramayana*, old old songs that had seen him through many births, marriages and deaths.

Towards me, mother was unforgiving. I was not to enter her room, nor use her comb, nor her chair or bed. Acne was venereal. She did not forgive father either: he was spoilt; his grandfather had given him money to visit whores; he was lust driven. 'Homosexual' was equivalent to 'hermaphrodite' or 'eunuch' ('hijra'). Mother called weak men 'hijra'.

Hijras cross-dressed, moving about in packs begging and singing. Though flat-chested, some carried infants to mimic motherhood. Their voices deep, their mannerisms slutty, they would display themselves if their performances weren't adequately rewarded. Some were ritually castrated at a mother-goddess temple, to be able to withstand women, to be the goddess herself. They were associated with Friday, fertility rites, weddings and births.

I'd go on long walks through Bombay. The sidewalks were jammed with hawkers. Pornography was sold wrapped in yellow cellophane and routinely titled Kama Sutra—an art and a science. I'd walk the Arcades under the office buildings around Flora Fountain, go past King George's statue on a black steed, walk up to the water at Apollo Pier where pigeons fed from the hat of the Prince of Wales.

A Jain taught me 'Karma'. My patience ran out: when I once shook mother by her shoulder, losing her balance she broke a hip joint never to recover. It was then that I tried suicide.

The trial was upon us. Father charged desertion; mother, cruelty. I stole billets-doux from my father's cupboard: 'I came running . . .' Sister discovered them in bed. 'To love is no sin,' the girl wept. Later sister tried suicide rather than testify against a father she loved. The girl was unintelligent, uncultured, unbeautiful. What did father see in her?

Mother was once vibrant and accomplished. She sang and played the sitar, among the first bourgeois girls to do so, since dance and music in old India were for temple prostitutes. During the freedom movement she wore homespun. She spoke to us of the astral body and the Lord to come. Why then had she given it all up? She was once beautiful. We found her tiny swimsuit in an old trunk. She was once offered a movie-role, or so she always said. Her father castigated her vanity. A silent-movie star, a neighbour, though disfigured in an accident, had photographs from her youth. Mother was too poor to afford a wedding portrait.

In quieter days mother would gather us around her and recite 'The Forsaken Merman' and weep. Among her letters we discovered a photograph of a little girl we didn't know. Mother had abandoned this girl because of us. Years later we saw the girl, a woman now, with long hair to her waist and wide eyes. Mother was not allowed to attend her daughter's wedding.

The wedding ceremony: The wife is separated from her husband by a screen, man from woman, matter from spirit. They are bound for life by the strength of a thread that circles seven-fold, a charmed circle of marriage. They are showered with rice.

Sister bowed before grandfather. Dressed in white and gold she wept.

My mother felt guilt for forsaking her husband and child. A Zoroastrian versed in Burmese magic had been contracted by my paternal grandmother to separate father from mother. Enchantments to fight enchantment: a charm only works if the victim is first told about it.

Since I wasn't allowed to go to the cinema in childhood I started watching all the old films I missed. I particularly remember Nargis, photographs of Monroe, the young Novak in *Picnic*, *The Children's Hour*: 'Look! I'm a freak with six fingers!' Without Bengali I sat through all of Satyajit Ray. I noticed the difference between the person and the screen personality in several Bombay stars. Kalpana, a neighbour, seemed more beautiful off-screen. Our disbelieving maid announced the star's breasts were foam rubber. I attended Kathak recitals, wrote poems.

Indians are divided fourteen times into fourteen languages. I studied my mother tongue first. English was taught under the rubric of 'General Knowledge' in the vernacular schools. Hindi is spoken in Bombay's film world. The school syllabuses were heavy with Victorian poetry. Babu English was the norm for daily intercourse. The Western-educated Indian of my age has no memory of any language other than English. If 'Black' expression is now the rage, India's foreign-educated elite lacks a language for it. It is true that I curse in Gujarati but it is equally true that I dream in English. Literary prose is more of a drawback to the Indian writer in English than his lack of Indian languages.

One day a little misshapen old lady followed my father into the house. Mother was hospitalized. A younger woman followed. They were my paternal grandmother and aunt. I had seen them for the first time at eighteen. They had forgiven father now that his marriage was irretrievably broken. My grandmother, an educated young widow, had become a small bent shape harbouring a twenty-five-year unforgiveness based on her 'principles'. I saw her one other time: 'To America! To America! To study English,' said my father's mother. It was the second time I had seen her. She was a devotee of the Meher Baba. When father fell ill in his childhood, his mother, a physician's widow, took him to the Baba for faith healing. Only an emergency operation saved his life. I was fearful of the mysterious Baba in childhood, dreaming of him before falling off to sleep. I had seen the barred cave where he meditated. My grandmother, a jeweller's daughter, was to leave her legacy to Baba. Father would not be forgiven.

The trial started. I accompanied mother to the Bombay High court: dark stone buildings full of pigeon droppings fallen from the rafters, with post-Raj liveried doormen, cloaked lawyers and their devils. Accusations of influence peddling, deception in marriage and divorce. All the old hurts and wounds photographed, catalogued, filed away, now played upon in the hands of paid lawyers. Mother refused an out-of-court settlement. She wanted 'justice', a public validation of the worth of her tribulations; he, a public absolution of his guilt, a public statement of male power. My old grandfather, weeping silently, sent away. They had certified my maternal grandmother insane, had her beaten with chains to drive out the devil in her. These forces once before judged my mother guilty of deserting a man she was forced to marry in an arranged marriage and whom she had the courage to leave. The same forces now called her a man-wrecker, an insane person, an undutiful wife, a thief of her husband's wealth, guilty of beating back a man who assaulted her. I testified on mother's behalf. We had become too poor to eat amid plenty. My parents who were married in seventy-five rupees spent thousands on their divorce. The trial had become mother's raison d'être: she spent years writing brief upon brief. A year later she was dead.

Minoo from the Drama Club wished to write a play on mother.

I gave language and history lessons. My students had interesting mothers: one loved her brother-in-law; another, an ex-baronet's wife, paid up her losses at the races by selling off inherited Chinese ivory—her house was full of pedestals on which statues once stood; a third, a Jew married to a Hindu film director, had a daughter from a previous marriage who dreamed of a career in the movies; yet another, the workless wife of a successful executive, concocted a life for herself as a stewardess.

Mother reprimanded both my girlfriends and the men, if they called me on the phone at home.

At nineteen I met Placid, twenty-five, bronze-complexioned, of middle build but athletic, with light eyes and a prominent mole on his cheek. He was a nuclear physicist. We met in a train and kept trysts each Tuesday morning. Sounds of children outside would waft into the room. He would await me wearing nothing but a towel wrapped around his waist, open the door to his one-room dwelling a crack to let me in. I wrote him poems; the scent of his sandalwood oil stayed with me days. Once, while he was visiting his family in South India, I turned up at his door and was seen by a cousin of his. I was severely admonished later by Placid.

I met a chef. The monsoons had set in. My friend wore a raincoat and dangled a cigarette from the corner of his rather full mouth, like Bogart. We took a cab to the sea and awaited nightfall. We made love: throat, chest, navel, thigh. The sky grew dizzy: 'What happened?' The cabbie watched the whole scene from a parapet. I was twenty; I had met the man in the train at fourteen.

Mother offered me a holiday in Kashmir. A Kashmiri curio-dealer had me locked into his offices and beaten, calling me an 'Indian' all the while because I had accidentally scratched one of his curios while handling it. I did not realize it then but I had internalized the pleasure of being beaten while watching all my mother's suffering.

During a famine, after waiting hours in a ration queue, I was charged the black market price. 'Ask your father how he got rich,' said the grain dealer.

I asked mother to leave me her papers. She refused: 'You will malign me.'

I read about a liberation movement among American homosexuals, the Mattachine Society. 'Mattachine' in Spanish means 'puppet'. After securing admission to a California college, father and I struck a bargain: I was to sign over to him everything in return for a year's fees. I signed transfers for half an hour. I felt free; I thought of never returning again.

I reported a boy-servant to the police for petty theft. I sat there listening to his cries as they tried to beat a confession out of him at the police station.

Mother appeared in the doorway on crutches: 'Do not leave. I'm about to die.'

Love is a constant terror of loss

The first loss of earth is loss of home.

II

The Dead Sea
Education: America, Germany, 1968–1976

The birds of paradise on campus were beautiful. The smog was sickening. Sister on long-distance line daily from Michigan. Food came in trays on a receiving line. Everything was antiseptic. Ravi Shankar, marijuana and male sex were considered liberating. A footballer in a bed sheet for a toga asked me to bed. An Indian bedecked his girlfriend as a Bengali bride in sandalwood paste and asked her to share a bath.

'Californication' he called it. Father wrote a letter a day inquiring about the identity of sister's lovers. I finally replied. Tom Bradley lost his first race to become a Black mayor. The Mazdaists of California turned out to be Christians in magian dress. Dr Bode of Westwood promised to convert sister's friend to father's satisfaction.

The friend sister was escaping decided to follow her to California. David had once been a priest. My sister lay curled up like a foetus when once I saw them in bed through a glass window.

The Dead Sea

At Christmas sister in India shot herself. Would elder sister leave everything and be by father? Younger sister had concealed the weapon from father when he threatened suicide and had used it against herself in a moment of complete isolation. 'I dragged her out of death's mouth,' mother wrote.

David and I went to San Francisco. It rained throughout the holiday season. Being suburb-bound I tried to connect with the sea again but lost my way. David tried looking up a father he had never seen in a phonebook. His mother said he was a trombonist with the Symphony. David did not find him. One night in bed I felt attracted to my sister's lover.

Carmela: Unlike mother she divorced the man she married young and deeply loved rather than suffer his negatives. She had eloped a week before high-school graduation. She displayed Italian verve. John stood by her through her mother's death, about whom she seemed to have guilt. They had a beautiful split-level home in Pasadena which she gave up. She received no alimony. She saw her children through their difficult adolescence: Tony had difficulty finding himself; Alex, a child genius, created a world of translucence around him with fluorescent paints when placed in a home for distressed children; Lisa had taught in Venezuela and lived then with a Harvard-law-school graduate; little Victoria grew up to be a lady. She was liberal and brought Alex to a showing of *Rosemary's Baby*: a film about selling one's wife to the devil for worldly success. When I asked her gruffly to type for me she countered that she wouldn't. Blood drained to my feet Carmela remembers. But we became friends.

I sought a homosexual roommate as I needed a guide. The first day we made love all day on the floor, moving from the parlour to the study, then to the kitchen and finally the bedroom. Michael had fallen in love with me. He took me to my first Hollywood gay bar. A 'girl' on the dance floor lost a ping-pong ball, that was serving for a breast, during a fast dance. Michael liked Black men. They liked me but I felt threatened by them. It was chic to have a Black friend then. I had my first experience of waiting mutely in a gay bar for hours. Michael himself had been first brought here on a religious anti-vice tour.

Scottie's: Scottie collected fees from a window; $1.50 then. I was introduced. We went to a locker room and changed into towels. Corridors were designed as a labyrinth to add excitement to the chase, and lined with cubicles holding planks nailed wall to wall serving as beds. Some had mirrors to separate the actor from the act or to double the pleasure. No names are ever exchanged. Scottie's clientele was young. The man with the shaved chest was from Antioch College and told me Christ's twelve disciples were his lovers. I spent the night fully dressed in the television room. The next morning I had my first quarrel with Michael.

The Dead Sea

I visited Scottie's three nights a week; it was life within the whale-belly. He had moved into a huge new place with a sauna, showers, game rooms and a restaurant. It might have been a bordello that went out of style. The orgy room had a vast bed: I was a prostitute soliciting clients. Someone kissed me feverishly. One could barely discern faces in the lightless room. I tried to satisfy everybody. A blonde boy patiently awaiting his turn brought a warm mouth upon me. It was over in minutes. I reached for him, but he fled. The metaphor for the gay life had been established. Once two sumo wrestlers in bed: unbearable stench of excreta and Vaseline.

At Easter we visited Michael's parents. Michel was ill with syphilis and I was sworn to secrecy. His father took us communal bathing. I felt strange that fathers should want to appear before their sons in uncovered nakedness.

When I touched Jane's breast she repulsed me. Later she was to sunbathe naked before me but I didn't respond. Her parents were John Birchians. They detested Communism since they had 'made it' on their own. They had built their house literally with their own hands. Their friends in Pebble Beach tried to indoctrinate me. They were against the Grape Boycott, Cesar Chavez's crusade for better pay for migrant workers. Eat the forbidden fruit, they said. When her mother read Jane's diary she sent her to a psychiatrist and found solace herself in politics. One morning I found her sitting on the toilet devouring *Portnoy* and bonbons, orating on obscenity to her husband in the bathtub.

Embarcadero Y: last night in California. All night riding elevators to new floors, new rooms, toilets, showers; new boys, nameless. After the morning shower I made love to a young sailor. A retired army man bent again and again to kiss a herpes sore on my inner thigh. Young soldiers maimed in Vietnam were a delicacy at Scottie's.
 Topless/Bottomless: a nude on a reflecting glass-top table, with older men looking up at her. My first view of a mature woman.

Carmela, in a goodbye gesture, bent low as Hindus do. I noticed the airport concrete painted green to simulate grass. The last night in California I dreamed an irate landlady demanding payment. Her husband held up to me a handful of hailstones. 'Glass!' I'd said.

Mother died. Her last letter reached after news of her death; I burnt the rest. 'He'd have been happy had I died' said father of me in a letter to sister. Sister told me mother was pregnant before marriage; this was the child that died.
 They laid my mother on a stone. Birds in the well ate her.
 At P.U. I had to properly delouse myself; my friends went into a frenzy of laundering.
 A character in a novel described as 'drooling in her panties

each time a man passed her' reminded me of mother. I held one should prove the love read about in Shakespeare.

Virgil had a no-nonsense approach to literature. He was a navy man, jazz trombonist, and a mathematician. He had written on Hollywood in literature. To him I was a son.

Nightly from ten to two I walked the streets, round and round the courthouse across the river. Chrome and glass living was too clean, the night walk was pain, suffering, work, time-killing self-denial, ecstasy. Someone screamed an obscenity; I was hardened in the pursuit of a night's lover. I wouldn't patronize the bar by the railroad track for fear of discovery. I counselled divorced men, drunks, bums I picked up, and received obscene phone calls.

Jal and Zenobia gave me food, shelter, advice, good music, love, but they could not keep me from the streets. He was quiet, she, vivacious. She was growing with his support. She knew no other men. She never threatened him. After the traumatic death of a wealthy father she had found stability again in marriage. Hers was a protected world and she wished for her friends what she most valued. I babysat their son, then four years old. Both father and son were Cancerians; they worshiped their mothers. What I wanted, however, was bliss; and bliss is antisocial.

At school Neville was taken to be an Eskimo. He refused to speak Gujarati or relish curry. He refused to sleep each night as it meant separation from his mother. His first separation came when his friend Chris moved to another town. He threatened to run away from home once when curry fumes got to him. He loved animals. Once he asked his mother if she would marry me since I alone of all men was allowed into her bedroom. Once he came back from Sunday school terrified by tales of brimstone and hell-fire.

I showed up at a party with kohl-lined eyes. Everyone thought me mad. I dreamed castration dreams. Crossing the town's river was crossing Styx.

The artists' fascination for homosexuality is explained by their fascination for bliss; homosexuality being blissed against the finality of reproduction. However what life seeks is pleasure and pleasure is tragic. Proust's life best exemplifies the distance between ideals and the lived life.

A racing-car driver—'Call me Joe'—picked me up and ordered me to mount him. He was massive, at least 200 lbs. The August moon. Five in the morning. Chill. Without a shred of clothing in the fields. I fell asleep. 'Stars! as in Phantom comics.'

I felt myself raised and dropped. I had blacked out and awoke on a thickly carpeted floor. 'Arabian Nights!' My face swelling from the blows. Men were going to work, eight in the morning, stepping over me on their landing, lying there shirtless. 'Please open the door, lady.' GOD IS

A FAIRY WHO WEARS A KIMONO AND PLUCKS HER EYEBROWS.
'I am Sgt Flood. May I know the story?'
I made one.
Inspected for rape.
'The lady you called on is praying for you.'
I chase a friar come to console me out of my hospital room. Anaesthetics. Silence. Darkness. Stitches. Light again. Why am I alive?
It was not my body they made love to. Everything that happened happened to another person.

Letter from a friend:
Leave the man who is mending you whole alone.
Ring down the curtain on your act. Blanche du Bois was my part.
Friends did not invite me over any more:
—If little Bobby should ask us what you are, what should we say?
—Tell him the truth, Ma'am.
Zen: The art of not going insane, committing suicide or becoming a cripple.
The therapist was sympathetic but remote. Once he was at the cinema with an older woman.
—Was that your mother?
—No, my wife.
He asked me to go straight: 'An inexperienced woman

will be paired with you at the Sexual Dysfunction Clinic. It's expensive.'

'Ten strokes of the bull-headed stick for lying; twenty for desecrating one's mother; fifty for desecrating oneself.'—A Pahlavi Text.

'I am Rimbaud, Baudelaire, I am Christ.'—Hart Crane.

Picked up a migrant Chicano labourer who robbed me and gave me a broken nose. A therapist, a Chinese–American girl, asked me to turn myself in to the police. She later eloped with a professor who left his wife and children.

A young female therapist at a crisis centre initiated my cure: 'You are not ill. You are free to go.'

Gay Liberation. I paid my dues. Silk scarves, overalls, tiny blouses, vests, jewellery, eye makeup, slimming diets, long hair, daily shaves, Garbo hats, heeled shoes. Protest marches, lectures, seductions: Are you a voyeur? Screaming in pain: an alien without rights. Disco dancing with Indianapolis Blacks. No one would pick up 'a queen'.

Boys sought me out for their first sexual encounters.

A married professor with children who finally decided he was gay brought his wife to interview me and find out what homosexuals were like. I was flattered, she wasn't.

Received my only ever love-letter from a literature major: 'I want you to pierce my centre . . . I want you to make the circles dance.' I did. The letter went on in that vein for four pages. We were all amused by it.

Len photographed me in the nude; Nancy, with 'props': a Jerusalem cherry in midwinter.

Len was a Southerner, from a family of tobacco-growers; in his ways were the tang of the Southern red earth, its gently lush vegetation and kindly manners.

Marty painted foggy pastels. 'What was the pattern on his back/Its features made and pressed?' He showed up for dinner at midnight. I chain-smoked and chain-brushed-my-teeth to sweeten my breath. He would lose class among his 'butch' friends if he slept with me. I had to give him up. He had given up painting for a factory job. His mother blamed his girlfriend.

After walking the streets I would listen to Tchaikovsky's Violin Concerto till dawn. Once I had refused to listen to music. It was my father's world. He and elder sister would stay awake in the darkness listening to Mozart. It was a world I wasn't allowed to enter. A world father and daughter shared. Heard Boulez conduct *Daphnis and Chloe*, as if the spirit was brooding upon the first waters. Mahler became a passion and the opera. 'Ah Lucia of the fountains/Walking the grass/a starling in each eye.'

Landini's 'Lament of Tristan' reminded me of strains my mother sang. No one played Chopin like Guiomar Novaes or sang like Moffo or became the mad Lucia like Callas.

I slept days and stayed awake nights to music. I couldn't sleep after seeing *A Clockwork Orange*. Fell asleep with the first light to awake in the afternoon to Josephine Jacobson reading on the radio: 'All need is dry / Rain is a metaphor.'

I admired my teacher. He was a poet and the first to commend my writing. Once, when I fell out of favour with him, I dreamed I walked to a bridge, stripped, stood on the parapet, decided not to leap into the river, stepped down, dressed, walked home. 'Only smile at me, sweet friend.'

Father sent sister over from India. 'She's sleeping with the chauffeur,' he claimed. She befriended an American, became pregnant; elder sister forced her to abort. Youngest sister was forced back to father, who had remarried secretly.

Elder sister herself had been four years with David. He wouldn't work, wouldn't go on Welfare; father had stopped all payments, so sister was forced to wash windows to support herself and David.

Carmela offered help: co-convicts' sympathy for each other. I sent sister $400.

A troop of the town's transsexuals arrived: 'It's your turn.' I discarded drag, dressed straight. They had taken me to drag shows they put on in Kokomo and at 'The Door', a drag-club in Indianapolis where Tania Tyrel, a Black, was billed as 'the first live sex-transplant in Indiana'. The operation was expensive. The cost was usually paid by boyfriends, who were later dumped; or club managers, from whom the girls 'defected' to escape virtual bondage.

The 'splice and push' operation created a vagina. Hormone therapy, silicone treatment, electrolysis and psychotherapy were supposed to create a brand new woman out of 'the soul trapped within the body of a man'. Ten years of experience showed the new person no happier then when he first started out and the project was abandoned. A phoney way of creating phoney men and women as cure for a sickness that doesn't exist.

Mark, at five, started dressing hair. His father was alcoholic; his mother remarried. His grandmother never forgave his mother. Mark spent time with his grandmother, who buried husband and sons and taught Mark the Bible. A brother, also gay, sought a gay marriage in Amsterdam. Mark lived in fear of society but he stood by the transsexual Michael as he stood by me. Having worked all his life, unprovided for by those who should have cared for him, Mark finally abandoned his lucrative profession and tried living off a 'lover'.

Chanced on *The Diary of Anaïs Nin*: 'Make stories out of your pain.' Anaïs Nin and I started a correspondence: 'Those who accuse me of narcissism do not know the meaning of the term. The contrary is proved by the letters of thanks I get from women I have helped.'

Danielle reads Anaïs Nin to me over the phone: 'Angels live not in the sky but at the bottom of the sea.' Danielle had the 'Golden girl Disease', anorexia nervosa. Her husband, Daniel, wrote on the Clown. She was a food-faddist, a compulsive smoker, an impossible neurotic and a generous hostess, and had an instinctive and deep appreciation of poetry. Her father died of malaria in Indochina; her mother never remarried. Danielle died at twenty-nine of cancer. 'Something broke within me, I cannot pray anymore,' her mother wrote to me. Danielle's husband turned to religion. One Easter Daniel sent me the elegy I'd written on his wife's death the previous Good Friday. Maybe all art is such a recall, a call beyond the grave.

Tennessee Williams arrived an hour late for a banquet, supported by two aging ephebes. He staged a highly derivative, two-character play revolving around a brother and a sister called *Out Cry*. He spent the evening conversing with a blond freshman ('I'm not a fag') who thought he was Tom from *The Glass Menagerie*. He was too drunk to talk.

Williams's autobiography catalogues the decay of an aging queen. It is a sad spectacle.

An angel exudes unblinking strength, but as death approaches the strength departs and blinking becomes incessant. Here are the five greater signs: the once-immaculate robes are soiled, the flowers in the flowery crown fade and fall, sweat pours from the armpits, a fetid stench envelopes the body, the angel is no longer happy in its proper place.

—A Buddhist text

Cruising: The stalls were partitioned from head to calf-level by polished stone panels. Contact was made by passing notes between stalls. Young flesh was prized and fought over. Boys knelt for each other. Faces were never seen. In the moment of orgasm one faced the bare wall. This was pain, joy, sorrow, absolution. People did it for years: main floor, ground floor, basement, fourth floor.

Sgt Flood of the vice squad lured people, asked for secrets of the gay world, prosecuted and sentenced gays for other offences like shoplifting or drug taking. He solicited me once but I eluded his net. Closet queers left messages on toilet walls. They suffered more from loneliness than exploitation.

The other alternative was keeping a lover.

The cynic as lover: Ken hated literature, society, himself and love. He looked beautiful; I desired him. I loved to watch him swim and shower. But he hated the woman in himself, hence the woman in me. He lived by projection, destroying in others his own hated selves over and over. He was ashamed of his origins: his parents were of the honest, hard-working middle class whose work ethic did not square with his cynicism, laziness and false success-values. He hated life-sustaining illusions and destroyed the illusions others created. But he himself lived in a fantasy of furs, expensive clothes, perfumes, make-up, even plastic surgery. His idea of woman was Elizabeth Taylor. He would not sleep with me. I tried not to be jealous: 'What you give others is not taken from us', but he smuggled boys into my rooms; I went to work to support him, he went cruising. Sgt Flood had him jailed for shoplifting. I tried for his release.

Ken appropriated my Indian costumes, gave my poems to his other lovers. He stole credit cards from his ex-boyfriend. I let Ken stay for seven months. I was seeking salvation, the soul's salvation. I felt guilt for once having turned on friends who supported me. I needed punishment for this just as I had paid off my guilt at assaulting mother by the subsequent assaults on me. Maybe I was re-enacting sister's relationship with David, mother's with father. I saw my young self in Ken and wished to protect him. But he was a cynic because there was no core to his being. I believed in literature, so he made his life into a fairy tale. I believed in Freud then; so he manufactured imaginary hurts and neuroses to explain away his cruelty. He was lost. He betrayed me to his parents: his father condemned me, though his mother appreciated the insight and understanding I offered her. She was a brave woman, from a family of coal miners, who read the books I sent her and was willing to undergo psychotherapy. My role as suffering Madonna had found a fit antagonist in Ken.

The poems speak of a beautiful illusion. Arturo Vivante quoted Dante to me: 'He who having loved love itself, loving pardons.'

Bridgeport came with its seabird calls, its Puerto Rican population, its Shakespeare Festival, and a New York actor, Daniel. He had his New York life: children's theatre in Central park, transcendental meditation in the sauna, theatre parties, roles for sexual favours, offers of payment for his body, trips in hydroplanes that he bypassed. Private meeting became a public act. We saw Julie Christie and Lillian Gish in *Uncle Vanya*: 'We shall live together dear uncle and work. Work.' Sonia's last scene. A young Chicago actress, Susan, was also in love with Daniel but he didn't respond. She admired Gish and we went backstage; the older actress had a purity of features others lacked. Julie Christie, in her small chemise, topknot and small presence, was different from what she was when she played Helena in trailing skirts and bouffant wig.

We set my twenty-sixth birthday, 5 November, for a meeting. Susan talked all morning: She couldn't act after an abortion; guilt at abandoning the mother-role for a career. The day before, I had read my poems publicly for the first time. We partied late. Susan knew she was my first woman, was very tolerant and kept a sense of humour. I clowned around as a dragon slayer. I delayed the final moment as long as was possible. Susan herself was an artist of the delayed moment of pleasure. She took three hours to undress: the hose, skirt, shirt, panties. I wept after love making. We bathed together. While she slept I celebrated her in a poem: woman, actress, girl, goddess, a temple, a fissure in the earth,

America: my Newfoundland. Worship changed to distance, which changed to hatred and finally indifference. When I last called Susan on the phone she was living with a Jewish actor and had had another abortion.

Victoria, daughter of a Greek city councilman, asked me to her room to dance wearing her brassieres, earrings and a fez. She would not touch me but allowed me to bring her off manually. Friends who saw us together told me she acted as if she were in love with me but I was unaware of this. At a party she showered all her guests with cologne. Her Greek father recalled her to Greece.

Frances, another father's daughter, was beautiful. She tired of macho men and hence wished for friendship with me. She accepted my worship and poems but refused love. Her boyfriend followed her from Arizona and Frances was happily married. The boys were saved their agonies. But when she wished for friendship with me after marriage Virgil counselled caution.

A student's mother complained to the dean of women, (an ex-Navy officer) when I taught *Tropic of Cancer*. My students were summarily taken away from me. My colleagues protested. The chairman of the literature department gave me a hearing. I offered that scientists who failed were lauded but any failed experiment in literature or pedagogy was castigated. I further stated very plainly that I could not teach anything that I had not found to be true in my own life. 'Nothing worked for me. I had to invent everything.' My students were given back to me.

A professor's wife spoke to me of infidelity to her husband. Hadn't I seen her visit the writer, my neighbour? No, I hadn't. Her husband tried to suppress my discussion of love in the literature department. They had two grown sons. She was committed to a marriage that had yielded no sensual pleasure for twenty years. I counselled divorce. She had admired me for my courage in living openly in a small town. Her friends sent her for a physiological check-up (the old culprit—menopause) and to a psychologist. No one thought of offering the same suggestion to the husband. He was a liberal. But he bullied his wife into staying married to him. I encouraged her to read her poems publicly. The writer published a story about their love. Mushrooming gossip noted the end of an affair rather than beginnings. She wrote me a poem:

> Quick brown hands
> Begin to explicate the abstruse text
> Our world is cornered
> We must turn it over
> Make it yield
> To our two curving palms
> And cry and cry each dusk
> Coax the east to rise to us

And shape a rounded light
If night should come again
Gentle now we shall sway
Like seaweeds or the heads of swans

A few years later her husband died of a brain tumour and she brokeoff her friendship with me. Along with Virgil's girlfriend, I consider her symbolic of the American woman in transition.

Virgil's girlfriend brought music to my life. Hers she filled with work. She rechristened herself Merry-less and lived alone. One Easter she left groceries on my doorstep: 'Now you and Anaïs have a love feast.'

My sister had now parted from David, who had become a successful banker. She lived with Paul but wouldn't marry him. It was as if Ariadne was confused between Theseus and Dionysius and the Minotaur, her true husband. But she recognised her thread. She came out of the labyrinth. I was glad for her. Although she had to undergo an illness first. (I was not by her in her illness.)

Sister encouraged me to go to Switzerland to see a lover I had picked out of the 'Personals' in the *New York Review of Books*. For some time I had feverishly responded to gay ads in *The Advocate*. Several masturbators on long-distance lines responded. I also had been offered a subservient wife-role by a Los Angeles accountant, Hindu philosophy at Blue Island

(Chicago), a pornographic love-existence in Waukegan, and a Pacific haven by a Berkeley professor: 'As I write whales pass by my window.' I chose the Swiss, a petty diplomat who described me as 'a mandrake' on seeing me, claimed to be involved in the sale of the century (of military hardware) and evicted me from his hotel room exactly after one day.

III

The Sea of Fertility
Travel: Middle East, 1976–1979

I was offered a teaching position in a West Bank College, in Israel. My life in America was over. I had tired of living in literature. I left without taking the degree, the book on Nin unstarted. Virgil spoke:

I too have fired and have been fired upon. I have lived with bums. I still have family pictures from the wallet of the Japanese I killed in battle.

Think of others.

I left for Jerusalem.

I was travelling in no-man's-land. The Dead Sea. The Sea of Fertility.

Rootless and homeless men are whisked by the Boeing 747 from place to place in luxury.

Permits and visas are written in Hebrew so the Arab won't read them. Every applicant is suspect. First the door phone, then the desk behind bulletproof glass. The Consul is out of sight. Once, a chance contact on the Consul's own direct telephone line. If you circumvent him, the border guards will be on duty. They carry guns but their superiors too are veiled from view. Sometimes they let loose huge friendly dogs who sniff everything from postage-stamp glue to loose-leaf tea. They could extradite one for fantasy.

No. Someone said no. 'You're $30 short. You cannot enter Jerusalem.' My wandering had begun.

A man fed me water in the desert.

Jerash, the dead city. The theatre of blood-red stone. Once they had much water here.

Venus is said to have come out of the sea at Cyprus. Penelope, who lost a plantation in Zaire and a home in Kyrenia, ran a hotel in Nicosia. Her husband planned dream houses.

The Phaeneromeni Mother giving suck; iconed.

Provincetown: The artists rejected me. Between husband, friend and children, Kathleen Spivack, the poet, was kind to me: 'I can enter your world.' Arturo could not help.

Ann, a painter and school friend was now living with Jim, an older artist of some repute. Ann had lost her father and tired of young men. Jim was famous for his silk screens of the full moon. A rare eclipse of the moon occurred just then and they travelled to the Dunes to see it. Ann was rediscovering Monet and she asked me to sit for a portrait. She had brought along Maggie the cat with her from Indiana so Jim indulgently built her a louvered window decorated with full moons, of course, so that she could let herself out of the studio whenever she wished.

My life became the history of rooms I inhabited: the completed home I was ready to leave because it was completed, the hotel room in Nicosia where I entertained Greek soldiers, the unheated wood-panelled room by the sea where I dreamed of reggae musicians being flogged, a friend's house which was more like a boat with its glass windows on the vast water and its birdcages, my Arab dream-room hung with carpets, the rooms in Hotel Albatross, Athens with its bellboys, a converted box room near Heathrow where I had nightmares of burning planes.

In London I read European poets in translation. I saw Blake's prints, Brancusi's sculpture; the lifeblood of English poets preserved at the British Museum. This was no mummery. At the Portrait Gallery the young Virginia Woolf: 'What can I say of the Parthenon? That my ghost came to greet me. A young girl of twenty-three with her life before her'; the hero T.E. Lawrence, thin and shrivelled; Richard II, puzzled and confused, the vital and tuberculotic D.H. Lawrence. I saw the films of Kenneth Anger with Anaïs

Nin and friends. Since the controversial sound track was withheld the film gave a feeling of a slow silent movie. 'Who was it I heard drowning in my sleep?'

I preferred Anaïs Nin's Louveciennes to Versailles. I dreamed Anaïs took me by the hand and we gently flew over the grass. Another time she appeared, cape and all, sitting on an American picnic bench conjugating the verb 'to make'. A rain veiled her from me.

At the Notre Dame I felt my alienation from God, the first time in years I had entered a church.

The young pietà at St. Peter's reminded me of sister's sorrowing face.

Paris: The queens at the Orangerie. The Aerogare: aging businessmen stripping for aging boys, the Algerian with long eyelashes stroking himself to coming, the little ouvrier whose side pocket's slit lead straight to his cock, the tongue bath given me by a soft man with halitosis, the gigolo disappearing into 'Ladies' with a younger boy. 'Tu n'orgases pas?'

Privates that resembled Bogart's! Pierre taking me home to a display of a young ephebe with buttocks up front, telling me about haunting railway stations near the barracks on holidays when young soldiers went home; I dreaming I was a miniscule point falling and falling in dark space.

Jeanine was married to a comic-strip illustrator. His teacher loved Jeanine; who devotedly tended the teacher's dying wife. Her husband took to one of Jeanine's Portuguese girlfriends at her behest. When Jeanine returned to her husband he had begun to love his new love deeply, and though the girl left, their marriage had changed. Jeanine bought a stereo and studied tap dancing.

Heidelberg had a facade for a castle. It was unreal: Reality is real. Reality is unreal. Reality is both real and unreal.

Rene fell in love with me. He had a lover in Brussels: 'Always divide your love in two as protection against hurt.' I, for my part, fell, in love with Rene's friend Jurgen, who did not like me.

I spoke no German and went dancing nightly at the Whisky-A-Go-Go. Danced with the lesbian Traute to Samba Pa Tí.

In young Germany it is kosher to dance alone. I picked up a German phrase from a movie: 'Haben-Sie ein Einhorn gesehen?' I sat through three and a half hours of Pasolini's philosophy of sex, *Salo* in German, and loved *Kaspar Hauser*, the story of a lost boy whose mother did not own up to him.

Manfred told me about Berlin's bisexuals. They wear mascara and call themselves 'Softies'. Manfred, whom I met at Bridgeport, was the first male friend of my own age who wasn't gay. He was then studying for a doctorate in law, publishing a non-ideological Leftist paper *Carlo Sponti* ('Carlo' for 'Karl' as in Marx, and 'sponti' for 'spontaneous'), seriously studying the modern film, counselling German and immigrant labour on their rights. He negotiated with my employer who failed to get me work papers. His mother kept us in cakes and viands.

Morgan taught philosophy and was writing on Kant. He had been homosexual once. He was a popular teacher. He was exploited: working far too many hours for too small a salary. He had undergone Scream Therapy. A Chinese woman just jilted by a German loved him, and they were happy together. Winnie's lover had been lost to a Persian girl, so she was initially suspicious of me of me but I quickly put her at ease. When her German lover reappeared Winnie left with him for Paris and Morgan returned to the States.

A Thai student of mine had met his German friend in a Bangkok bar. My student had later rescued his friend when Saigon fell. In his turn the German invited the Thai boy to Germany when student riots broke out in Thailand. They showed me what gay friendship could be.

Dieter too was enamoured of Jurgen. As he gave me the description of his friend I suddenly realised he described the man I was smitten by. But I did not tell him lest it pain him. We made love: I reminded him of an Anglo-Indian friend of his in Cologne. He invited me to join the commune he lived in. Helmut, a blonde, bespectacled long-haired hippie, lived with Traute. They were the commune's 'parents'. Uli was a soft-hearted alcoholic. They all protected their patients at the old people's home from rapacious relatives. They listened to Dylan and Theodorakis. They gave me kohl-dust from Afghanistan. They refused me LSD.

Rene took me to the Symbolist Retrospective in Baden-Baden: Bocklin's 'Isle of the Dead', the golden Redon, Klimt's 'The Kiss'.

My German papers didn't come through.

Human beings dislike each other and themselves. A physical stench is emitted from our skins that we and others can't stand.

The unreconstructed Germany: Children of the war-wounded with war wounds, Rene among them; he'd never forgiven his father for returning from a POW camp when he was five.

The hippies offered me Greece. I needed connection.

Astipalea: O Thalassa! In every window the sea. From starboard and stern boys crying 'Dolphino!' Husbands dreaming in doorways, black-veiled women against white-walled houses.

Cos: Hippocrates' platane-tree, the Aegean. Pannaghia, the autumn feast of Mary, once the many-breasted Ephesian Diana. Processional dancing in an endless chain, humankind itself coming from an arched cave and going out endlessly. Soldiers on alert against Turkey. The wail of violins. Dancing the Shiftetelli, a Turkish harem-dance with George: starting on satyr goat-foot, progressing to moth-like wing movements of the hand, ending with a single pelvic thrust.

The Greek Church.

Paula invited me to her tent before her husband. I

assented and later regretted it. Had to learn to get along with people on an island.

The Villa des Mysteres at Pompeii. A satyr-like bearded Dionysus at the Naples Museum. The volcano and the Serene bay.

> With what spirit, what heart,
> What desire and passion
> We lived our life: A mistake!
> So we changed our life.
>
> —Seferis, 'The Denial'

'When a person enters a new phase of life such as joining the world as an adult, he feels impotent and retreats into the family for strength. Dreams of sleeping with one's parents or siblings are common at this stage.'

—Esther Harding

India. Mother was dead. I went looking for her. Wept again at the same window. Her kimonos, saris, polka-dotted kerchiefs, shoes, crutches, hairbrush, hand mirror, all disposed of. In every room a portrait of mother with a vigil lamp: it keeps ghosts from returning; more exorcisms of the guilt of the living. The sea outside. Birds still straying into the green house. The mango trees, the old rusty green gate, shed snake-skins. Gardener and watch-dog dead. Sunsets and flocks of parrots at dusk. A part of Eden changed and unchanging. I saw the moon set and the sun rise over the same curve of the sea one dawn. The heat and humidity.

Father lived on another beach. He made locks. Workers who had joined his factory as boys were now grown men, still at the same tasks. Once when I went to father's home in his absence his servant refused me entry. Father had married his girlfriend: a doll in a doll's house. I saw no feeling pass between them. She is Piscean. She told me of her life. She taught herself sewing to support a fatherless family. My father had taught her the alphabet. She longed for a child. She had become barren: after a miscarriage a quack had cauterized her with formaldehyde. Yet she forced my sister to give up her baby daughter. My father had made over his entire wealth to her. He had wanted elder sister to mediate disputes between him and his new wife as we had once done with our mother. Sister refused. He called his wife the same names he called my mother: man's hatred of woman. Father spent his wealth whitewashing fire temples, towers of silence and wells of the dead. His wife was a delegate to the matrimonial court. He intercepted my certificates in the mail in order to keep me home. They proposed I marry. Kathleen Spivack called India's family intrigues 'Byzantine'.

My youngest sister, a Piscean, had been alone at sixteen by mother's deathbed. In a delirium mother asked for her son, she called for her husband. Father who finally arrived after a whole day's telephoning sat on the veranda calling out 'Rosie, Rosie' in imitation of a neighbour calling her maidservant instead of rushing mother to hospital. It was again youngest sister who found our sister in a pool of blood after breaking into the bathroom where the girl had locked herself. After mother's death father starved sisters to break their spirit. Youngest sister played deceit with deceit. She went to a match they found for her in Iran, then broke the engagement.

My father rejected me because of my life.

Placid was not to be found again. He had given me a false family name and had moved.

My paternal aunt told me about their mother: One of twenty-one children, given away for adoption. Her new mother treated her well until she married and had children. Then the mother turned distrustful. Father was a dutiful son: I saw the sari border with peach, pear, pansy that he designed for his mother, the photo frames he made in carpentry class. 'We three will live together always,' he'd say. They had held him to his adolescent word. And confirmed stories of insanity in their family: an uncle kicked a cousin down a staircase to her death for rouging her face; grandmother poured boiling water on aunt because she eyed a boy. Aunt never married, living lifelong with childhood mementos: the Persian epic translated, in several volumes, her mother's wedding furniture, her father's British Dominion passport, my father's dolls, his gold-framed baby photograph, even his baby potty. She showed me the Chinese silk, embroidered in white on purple, that her grandfather had bought her, a dollar a yard, a part of the family jewellery she inherited and my father's boyhood watch, then one of two pieces in Bombay. She was in her brother's shade and couldn't accomplish much until he left. Later she trained in homeopathy: like to cure like. She accused my mother of selfishly luring a rich widow's son. They had pinned all their hopes on him. My mother's family accused father of irresponsibly luring a quietly married woman. She had left behind her entire dowry.

My natal chart:

Moon in Cancer, Pisces rising. Sign of the exile and the poet. Wealth is spurned. Success at thirty-six. Early death. Eccentricity lessens with age. Literary success, world travels, pilgrimages, a house by the sea. A twenty-year Venusian proficiency in the arts: aesthetic and sexual. Conventionally speaking a bad-charactered person but devoted to the learned, friend to society's rejects, sacrificing, attaining wisdom after repentance at Eros. Last years in decline. Friends are progeny. Beloved of women. Disappearance of an aged woman. Moon and Jupiter cushioning against poverty. Great faith in mankind.

Mother died intestate. Father refuses cooperation in freeing the estate from the law. My sisters quarrel; I fail to reconcile them. I dream mother cuts a golden snake into three: elder sister offers me her share of the legacy as 'a tangible proof of love'. The estate still lies unclaimed.

Minoo doesn't care any more for the theatre or for nostalgia. His father is dead: 'Are you waiting for the death of your father?'

Giving away my books and clothes I journeyed to the Dalai Lama in Dharamsala. 'Do not come to me in sorrow,' said the teacher. He was fat, squat and jolly. He had written of his life as a myth: 'When my mother was carrying me, circumambulating the temple she touched her forehead to the ground where sprang a flower.' His pedagogic secret: 'Do not give the Dharma to those not ready to receive it.' He never spoke in self-defence, nor ever displayed any doubt about the teaching. Meditation was not egoistic; it freed others. The Buddhist myth lived meant the monk's life. Religion was not aesthetics. Sonam, a young monk trained at Shantiniketan, helped me to reconcile myself to my self. They took away my pain: 'There is no "Why?" It is. That's Karma.' There is no destiny, there is character. Compassion meant allowing others their idea of themselves.

They revered my father, who sponsored my religious studies. Each evening the novices sit in a rock garden. They chant the Manjushri prayers. Each deity has a syllable. Manjushri's is 'HRI'; he cuts bonds, suffering, illusion. The chant is the throb of the heartbeat. Youths chant in polyphony. They clap their hands to cut connections with the day that was; Manjushri's single syllable articulated allows the soul flight just at the moment of sunset. It is a mortal sin to eye a monk. A hundred thousand prostrations. That is the beginning practice. How to dwell on earth. To see things as they are, to speak things as they are, to feel things as they are.

'The Tibetans teach you how to die'— Antonin Artaud

Kathak dancing with Leela. Lacked stamina but sensed a great freedom on tying bells to my feet the first time. I encouraged Leela to temporarily leave her master to perfect her dance in Delhi.

Mrs Nowrojee kept a sixty-year-old provision store filled with empty showcases and a whiskey ad, White Horse. A magnificent view from the store. Her husband kept old accounts, she somnambulated and an eighty-year-old mother-in-law wielded authority. They disapproved of the Tibetans and the travelling life.

An Indian doctor and I made love on trains and buses we rode out of town together to escape gossip. We had trouble establishing the male and passive roles. His society obliged him to ridicule me in public. Yet when he forsook me I followed him to the Punjab.

'Sorrow is inauspicious.'
'The cave of the heart is the seat of the intellects.'
'Love, feeling, make time real.'
—Swami Chinmayananda, *The Upanishads*

After I broke up with my friend I dreamed of a broken watch.

Heard Subbulakshmi sing Meera and saw Vyjayanthimala's recital of temple dances. Mrs Gandhi lost the election over sterilization. On my way home I stepped over the bodies of people sleeping on Bombay's pavements. In front of my parents' six-room apartment that the two of them used were thatched huts on the beach; entire families camped under the sky. 'I did not get rich by stealing from them,' father said.

Do something for the suffering people.

'I can do nothing': This is the artist's position.

I shut out all contrary evidence to the beautiful image of India, its art, drama, music, religions.

The Taj by moonlight, a surreal dream-image. Below, musclemen built their bodies by the river. At dawn a peacock fan-tail on an eastern gateway.

Anaïs Nin died. 'A healer lays hands on me and takes my pain away,' she had written. Father had asked her to influence me into returning home; she in her kindness had obliged him. 'May it all be a beautiful adventure': her last words to me.

My mother's father was stern. She wasn't allowed to wear pastel colours, nor flowers. The first of five daughters, she had responsibility early in life. 'She was ahead of her time. She wanted to lecture forty years ago when women kept to the house.' She had to fight to go to college. Accused of wanting to meet men she enrolled in a Women's University. Then she stood accused of befriending male professors. Women had to stay indoors during their periods, which were ritually considered unclean. Her neighbours kept exact count of mother's periods and each time ritually cleaned their

corridors throwing water after her as she came and went.
Tagore painted women at barred windows.
A younger cousin shows her sexuality refreshingly openly.

Gangtok: again the dancing lightning of the Tibetan Mass. A green rainforest light. Woman by the roadside breaking stones, her infant asleep on a pavement nearby.

Chitrabhanu—'God is a perfect human being'—was a friend I had made in Chicago. He lectured on vegetarianism movingly. He had answered my questions on sexuality with silence. Now he was married with young sons. My friend told me he had yogic self-control and could suck mercury into his penis. He had become a Jain monk at seven. He blessed me.

My stepsister: a mother of five, white-haired, a grass-widow for sixteen years to her husband's career in the merchant navy. She lived in phobic fear of ritual contamination and bathed compulsively. She talked of her parents' divorce blighting her girlhood; no one would marry her. She feared society. 'Mother was fearless.'

Nissim Ezekiel, an Indian poet, did not like my poems. He was courteous and kind.

A museologist, a teacher of mine told me: 'Give up your life. You can never teach here.' Invited to Tehran, I left India.

IV

Six yards of golden silk for Manfred's mother; textiles, jewellery, sandalwood for the hippies; gold and red voile for Carmela.

The stretch between the Eastern Mediterranean and the Hindu Kush is fabled: Baghdad, Basra, Samarkand, Herat, Kandahar, Ghazni, Swāt. When my German friends returned from Afghanistan with photographs I dreamed of the seven lakes of Bandi Emir.

At last in an Arab dream-room hung with a saddle bag, a lamp, camelhair carpets.

I dreamed a tauromachia with my lover as the bull.

My friend wanted to sleep with both my sister and me.

Once sister brought over a lover of hers to my room. The Persian landlord evicted me: 'This is not a brothel.'

Wept while reading 'The Wasteland' that same morning at a school. Later I read them from the *Cantos*:

What thou lov'st well shall not be reft from thee
What thou lov'st well is thy true heritage

Garden of Delight

The students wished me for a teacher but the American bosses would not hear of it: 'Your accent isn't right.'

I openly dreamed before the Persian boys I taught at college. They brought me their gifts and admiration. I read the Persian *Epic of the Kings*—Siavosh, the guiltless martyr.

A Persian film: The cure for a madman was marriage, to a prostitute. Tehran was full of them. They solicited trade in the streets. Once, a young Persian wished to sleep with me, but only along with a woman. He picked up three girls riding together. One sat with a child, another drove, a third haggled the price: Rls 3000 for all three, for the two of us for a night. I declined.

A visit to the brothels. The Madam auctioning off girls: '500, 400, 300'. No takers. The most expensive were young, dressed much as American coeds. A peddler came in selling clothes, jewellery. The women teased him. Wonder what happens to these men who live only with women due to reasons of business! A man and a woman sleep behind a green curtain. Let them be sinning forever!

A jealous co-worker spread the false story that I had slept with my students; something I never do, on principle. I did not deny my sexuality but was obliged to defend myself against false charges. I was dismissed with full pay for the remaining term of my contract. Rex (Reece), a gay liberation leader, wrote to me:

> You say I helped ease your lot for a while; you taught me to be pleased and happy to be gay. Just being with you I knew more than from all the rhetoric we used to spout. You are what it's all about, and your being fired and having 'to line your soul with steel' is evidence of that reality. They still can't handle your honesty, your simple truth. I feel humble knowing you, and honoured. Yes, Anaïs Nin is big (in Los Angeles). A friend (G.A. since he started with *Architecture Digest*—he's lining his soul with steel also—before that he was 'Morning Glory') had records of her reading. He used to pretend to be her. So we often had Anaïs Nin to dinner.

In my student room I wrote a book on Anaïs Nin in sixteen days. My sister, a stewardess, who had afforded me all my travels sent me books. For years I had thought I was Anaïs Nin. 'I is another.'

When a soldier visited me my Islamic students asked me to leave: 'You are worse than a bitch. You should live with wild animals in the mountains.'

Gregg Fitzgerald, a student of mine, published his haiku, 'Rain In Her Voice'. He speaks of the daily suburban reality of love, hurt, violence, repression, the changing prairie seasons, return of the beloved, a friend's death. He has modernized and Americanized the Haiku.

I made love to three Armenian boys. Read their history: the long bloody trek to Baghdad, their loss of self-respect due to persecution, the mass burial of a mountain of skulls topped by a bishop's hat.

In the dream the Other is the Self.
    The Indian doctor got married.
    My letter to Rene was undelivered. He had moved to Cologne.
    My German friends sent me addresses of Tehran bars from the *Gay Guide*.

On a visit to the Bazaar saw almost a child's impression of the Quaj'ar king, Fath-Ali Shah with navel-length beard, and a moustache, hand painted on wood: 'I want to be feared as a king and debauch in my youth and when I die I want to be revered as a saint.'

Heard of an Amman Sufi order from travellers: They concentrate on Allah's name (a mantra), they whirl and dance, and the Shaykh hits you on the chest, gently, on the left side.

Rumi and Shams-i-Tabrizi: Not until did Rumi lose

Shams-i-Tabrizi did he start pouring out his soul ecstatically in poems. Once, Shams threw away all of Rumi's manuscripts into a river. Rumi set up a hue and cry. When he gave them up for lost, Shams brought up each page from the water, intact and bone dry.

At the Zurkhané (House of Strength) athletes descend into a pit, like Mithra slaying the bull. They liked me but I was shy.

Tehran: a Gold-rush Frontier-town. The boys I slept with stole from me: cologne, underwear, jewellery, trifles. They were young, uneducated for any trade, usually unemployed. Wealth mattered; I was ridiculed for not holding down a job. Nobody read or cared for literature. Once we went without dinner to be able to afford tickets to a piano recital. The Iranian summer, laden with jasmine and orange, alive with solicitations.

Howard, Tehran '79
'Now y'all celebrate me!'

He's a water buffalo at a bath	Do my feet
A sex adviser	Do your thing
A money maker	Rake it in
A quick-change artist	What shall I put on?
A Vietnam C.O.	The Whiteman's your enemy

He coached a Crown Prince	Sharks will get the security men first
He has a Black mama	A wife, son, nephew, retarded daughter perhaps

Paul's grandmother was the last empress of China
Who looks like Divine who eats shit

Howard has stopped fighting
Howard has started living

A Tehran astrologer told me, 'You are Jonah; your sister, Daniel.'

Jonah had a pact with the whale: he would not walk out free and the whale would neither digest him nor spew him out.

I moved into a Youth Hostel, $2 a night.
Virgil wrote:
I wish to give up the academic and middle-class life at sixty. Now I understand the kind of terror you felt at a much younger age.

'Fuck Gauguin!'—Henry Miller, *Letters to Anaïs Nin*.

The artist is the beggar or the Buddhist monk in modern society. He fulfils a function; he makes the philanthropy of the rich man possible; he challenges the miser. He makes rebellion in the name of aesthetics. He keeps accounts. Finally, the capitalist marketplace absorbs him; his book is sold and bought; the bourgeoisie he baits take him to their breast and love him for being the spoilt child he is.

Manfred gave up politics. In the wake of terrorism, the German police curtailed civil liberties. 'I am declared an enemy of the state,' he wrote sadly. He now wished to be a student of the film director, Alexander Kluge.

Letter to Manfred:

You chose the way of Marx, I of Freud, Jung and the writers Lawrence, Nin, Barnes. Now you have learnt that art too is politics, that you will reach large numbers of people and the police of course will not understand your films.

I took my book to the States. Virgil urges publication. Call to Merrylees: 'I am proud of you.'

On a previous visit I had spent a night in New York and left on the same plane for Europe. Had shoplifted Nin's sixth *Diary*, spent a night at the Continental Bath—'Patrons with running sores, infected eyes, ears or nose, may not use the swimming pool'—and had nightmares about the many-headed dog.

Ken's mother intervenes. He will not see me. She tells me he still wears make-up but builds muscles and is going to Hollywood.

I definitely break with Daniel, in New York.

Jal easily picks up the thread where we left off three years before. Zenobia avoids me all summer. They now live the suburban American life; their son, now fourteen, an American kid. Jal has given up literature for administration.

Linda, a school friend, has married a composer who uses no longer used instruments like the glass harmonica. She has written on Kafka, Grass, Kosinski. A published critic, she is out of work. We grew close when I consoled her after the loss of her German friend. Her grandmother was a friend to Luckács in Hungary. Her aunt died in Hitler's gas chambers. I sent her an elegy on her mother's death. 'I liked to paint my mother's portrait but it came out like mud.' Though plain I felt attracted to her after years of friendship and Linda explained such a feeling was genuine.

Lost touch with Roz, a small-town Indiana girl, declared 'schizophrenic' after the break up of her first love affair. I would not sleep with her. She was to have married me to get me American papers. 'Now they have tubs for straight couples. I patronize the Great San Francisco Hot Bath and Tubs Co.,' she wrote. Engaged to a Chinese, who turned out to be married, I last heard she was in the Army pursuing a medical degree, which she wouldn't have been able to had her history of incarceration been known.

Revisiting the Chicago Baths I catch gonorrhoea, 'fires of love', 'morning glory' or 'pearl'. Easily cured.

'Newer and newer cures will be found but the fear will

remain. Syphilis will be the symptomatic disease of our civilization.'—Henry Miller, *Age of Assassins.*

Have to go to a South Chicago Free Clinic with pimps and whores. An immigrant Chinese doctor treats me. He speaks perfect American slang—'Spread your cheeks', and has never heard of Chinese alchemy—'What's that?'

Carmela has written me for ten years. Tiring of the secretary's life she has started a business recycling Society clothes: 'The wife of the director of Araamco gave me a dress worth $1500.' Her husband has had a leg amputated and lives alone in Westwood. Her daughter teaches now in China; her baby exclusively speaks Mandarin.

Ruth Ann welcomes me warmly, puts her house at my disposal and presents me her first published poem:

GIFT FROM HOSHANG
The small box unfolded a bell.
A calyx carved from six bronze petals
Rings of a Parsi rose
Infinite light in my hand
I thanked him, hearing echoes
Of changes rung, commands
For ritual quests and the rhythms of homely days
To wake, sing praises or to grieve

But he said: No
This is a dancer's bell
You must be the mover

Garden of Delight

But we lost touch again.

Gregg Fitzgerald is married. Single people make the best friends, fugitives also.

The impossible love affair with my sister, that I had transferred to Zenobia, is rekindled. On the last day we remained silent.

A dream of loaves and fish.

I wrote her a poem.

Freny and Jean Bhownagary picnic on the grass at Battersea on salmon and grapes. Freny walks with a cane—a knee injury—yet is still beautiful. The Indian artists F.C. Souza and Sabavalla had painted and sketched her portrait. We visit an exhibition of Japanese erotic art. Freny traces a line from the Japanese down to Toulouse-Lautrec. They have filmed Cambodian temples and will exhibit ceramics in Japan. Their friend, Satish Kapoor, asks me to recite from memory. He calls my poems 'Vaishnavite': an allusion to my love of cycles, circles, repetitions, reincarnations. Freny declares herself 'a Parsi Buddhist'. 'How come after such a life your poems are so pure?' she asks. They had become so international one barely guessed their origins.

Father gives me $500 towards the Nin book, and a Victorian guinea with St George on it.

Flight back into the Iranian Revolution.

Met a drunk man who displayed himself on a street during a blackout. We ran to his house hand-in-hand through the dark street to beat the curfew. He asked me to mount him. In the morning he showed me a huge portrait of his wife.

Blood, beatings, killings in the street. I lost innocence. 'Write your senator to stop the killings.' (The regime had links with the Senate, of course. I shouldn't have been so naive.) Asked an Imperial-Guard-turned-revolutionary if I could help: distributing leaflets, anything. 'No you're a foreigner.' 'Capitalist', 'bourgeois', even 'liberal' overnight became dirty words. Everyone suddenly wished to belong to the 'proletariat' or became 'radical'. I had become a generation older in a matter of months. My eyewitness account was published in a Bombay quarterly.

Lost my new job after the revolution. My boss, who had asked to sleep with my sister in exchange for a contract lost his job for being associated with the old regime. Under Islamic laws unmarried males may not teach women and homosexuals may not teach.

Moved to the Zoroastrian poorhouse. Homosexuals caught soliciting are executed by firing squads.

Revisit the fire temple. Ashes on forehead for humility.

'Two is the perfect number.'—*The Gathas*

Katharine: a horse-trainer-turned-English-teacher; an opium addict. Tells me she once worked as a prostitute outside

London. Her policeman father committed suicide when her mother, a lesbian, moved in with a girlfriend, a woman who beat clients for money. She lied about her lovers to her husband, 'to protect him', she said. Dishonesty as a way of life of the badly loved child. Their friends Florence and Louis shoot heroin first thing in the morning. Louis was imprisoned for trafficking in Tehran.

Nigerians in Tehran: independent, proud, gentle. 'They were slaves,' they said of the American Blacks. One complained about being picked as a sex athlete by women in Europe. Sex on the trains, etc.

Met Siamak at the Hare Krishna Restaurant.
　—What is God?
　—Two people, I say.
　I left him as he rejects homosexuality: 'I'm a most sexual person' he said of himself. He told me he had starved in Benaras, pushed drugs in Germany, visited a Delhi brothel in monks' robes, feigned madness to live free in a madhouse (he was discharged after a month), tried suicide by walking away into the desert east of Kerman, was certified 'schizophrenic' by army doctors and had stolen ashram property. The night of the revolution he stole bullets from the liberated army depots and gave then to people with guns in the street. He studied astrology in India: 'A four year transit of the Dragon's

tail. A yogi can get liberation then,' he predicts for me. He gave me opium.

   Kathleen Spivack writes:
   I am now divorced and living alone with the children.
   Money is always a problem.
   Survival, Survival.

Stanley Kunitz had voted her one of the ten best young poets in America today.

Sister sends me a $150 check 'as crisis fund'. I return it.

Joseph from Ananda Marga practices abstinence and urges me to do likewise. An ex-footballer from Reno, Nevada, he frequented whores: 'They were nicer than the girls at my Catholic school.'
   Those friendships formed in need can be understood only by those who have been in such need.

Juan. An echo of Ken. I feared him. There was something distant about him as in most dreamers. He came to my room to read books. I confessed my love. He equivocated like Penelope: 'I wish to sleep with a man in the future. Bisexuality is true liberation.' When I told him I definitely break with people who can't reconcile their friendship with sexual love he looked sad. So I decided to be his friend.

The poorhouse-room became vibrant when he moved in. I furnished it with mats, a rug, blankets given me by friends who had moved. I had two teacups, a kettle, a stove, a spoon. Juan bought a knife. We ate, slept, and bathed together. It was a childhood sexless love.

'I've slept naked with friends without having sex,' he said.

He spoke in a monotone and in monologues as if somnambulating.

He trembled reciting Baudelaire.

He had repudiated the University, studied philosophy, taught fishermen.

He idolized me. I broke the illusion. I demanded sex; talked openly and callously about my sex life.

I had an illusion of him as my lover: he broke that illusion.

The day was day again; books, books again; food, food. I felt a loss but also a freedom.

He withdrew into himself. Smoked hashish. He was Piscean.

'You live in a world of beauty and bruise yourself against the other's rim,' he told me. 'You're Anaïs Nin!' Each time he wished to leave I wouldn't let him. 'In living you hurt others,' he said—Ken's exact words, only Juan wasn't malicious.

I told him every story. He made no allowance for my past. There is no way to understand a childhood hurt except by suffering it oneself.

He said my autobiography was 'made sublime', that I wanted to present myself in a good light. To one's beloved one shows the potential self, the beautiful self, though I do not care for public opinion. Autobiographical art is suspect. All art is falseness not only in the sense that it is a moulding, a retelling but also in the sense that art is the hand-making of one's life; it is a made universe. Even autobiography is fiction. 'You are using me to write poems,' Juan said. 'What do you want, literature or love?' Virgil had asked. I would have rather lived peacefully. The invert in creating life destroys it. If our experience is destroyed our behaviour is destructive. But Juan taught me a respect for sex:

—You think I'm a puritan.

—No, sexual continence is a principle of conservation in the East.

Juan himself was trying to undo in himself the excesses of the sexual liberation in Europe meanwhile trying to liberate himself truly.

His grandfather was a nobleman who repudiated his heritage, went to Africa.

His father heads a European Art Foundation.

Juan's favourite word was 'harmony.' He did not take kindly to my pride, anger, defensiveness, jealousy, melancholia and emotional outbursts. There is a germ in us: it is called doubt. Self-doubt breeds anxiety. No love can withstand anxiety.

He came angry as Hamlet. He wished for purity, I thought. I thought he was angry at my sexual insistence. For a moment I saw him as Savonarola. Maybe I was projecting my own sexual guilt, my sexual frustration with him. He always talked of Platonism, of a higher beauty in male friendship. I thought, 'I now understand Hamlet's scene with Ophelia perfectly':

> Talking about food won't make you full
> Babbling of clothes won't keep out the cold
> A bowl of rice is what fills the belly;
> It takes a suit of clothing to make you warm.
> And yet, without stopping to consider this,
> You explain that Buddha is hard to find.
> Turn your mind within! There he is!
> Why look for him abroad?
> —Han-shan, *Cold Mountain* (T'ang Period)

—'You live in literature.'

We parted. I tried to break with him gently but firmly. But being sensitive he took that to heart and repudiated me: 'Do not try to search me ever again. Ever. For I will be gone and never return.' He was visibly trembling with emotion. 'Your love was a falseness from beginning to end.' He returned my poems: 'They are only words.' He returned all my gifts to him: 'I want no material link with you. You're mercantile. You gossip.' But he kept the first poem.

In a moment of complete isolation and bitterness I had confessed to a relative stranger my failure in spite of sharing food, home, books, money.

This reached Juan, fifth-hand, through Joseph. I wrote him a letter, which he returned:

You showed me how much the vocabulary of love partakes of the vocabulary of business: we invest in friendship, we reap profits, we suffer losses and so on . . . I wish freedom from this round of money and retribution through money. I consider myself generous. I hate pettiness in others. But for my generosity I do expect warmth and feeling in return . . . I never thought to 'buy' you. Attention is enchantment, luring, attracting, but the puritans see only solicitation not aesthetic beauty. Help in the world is always real, financial, practical.

I later learnt Juan had had an interview with the asexual Joseph of Ananda Marga: Mushrooming gossip had again recorded an affair's end rather than beginnings. Joseph was a scavenger, a squatter, one afraid to love, who partook vicariously of the loves of others, I rejected him.

Juan wrote me a note on the back of the envelope he returned:

My disgust over your behaviour towards other people is the origin of the grievance . . . You are repressed and frustrated—even if you boast of being 'free and liberated'—You don't want to control your own Ego.

'I is another.'

When he left, what I remembered of him I pressed into

these pages. Gossip had become aesthetic. I wrote him a sestina: he would smile each morning at waking and simply take up our talk about books or friends left unfinished the night before. At the spring new year he showered me with raisins. The night I decided to be his friend he kissed me goodnight and left to sleep in the hostel: 'You disagree with commerce. So you take up travelling. You pay to sleep. You pay to eat.' I saw his face illumined as many times before. Luminosity is a characteristic of nothingness (nirvana). But then this light was withdrawn.

I gave him the address of a Hinayana monastery in Ceylon. He decided on the Seychelles instead.

The image of the temples at Khajuraho: Outside, couples in erotic embrace, mad, easy, in abandon, in slavery to the body. It is all there, real, depicted. Within: the plain, empty, illumined reality of pure, passionless nothingness. The inside and the outside, the two sides of the same egg-globe, the temple and the cave. Juan restored for me this complementary aspect of purity and sensuality.

The mystical love: the love for parents, sisters, friends. Perhaps all our loves are only a pale reflection always of what glows at the heart of the universe; of the love of the outstretched arms on a cross.

La vida est Sueño: Perhaps all things are illusion, this

crying, this crumbling, this falling away, this vanishing, this revelation of that which is no more, and there is nothing given but this dream. This dream is not given but earned.
—Anaïs Nin, *Diary VI*

Asha Coorlawalla, modern dancer, student of Kathakali and of Martha Graham's, re-christened Uttara by Muktananda writes:

> Asha is the spiritual path.
> Uttara is the highest spiritual truth.
> Arjuna taught her dancing in the thirteenth year of exile as a eunuch dance-teacher. She was the king's daughter.

In reply to my Christmas poem Mulk Raj Anand writes: 'Do not forget the wisdom of the heart our mothers taught us.' He urges an autobiography so that the lyric impulse can suggest undertones. I write, in longhand, a diary in two days. The places I have passed through are places on no map.

Hoveida: thirteen years Iran's Prime Minister. He could have escaped as others similarly incriminated did during jailbreak on the day Tehran fell. Instead he chose to turn himself in. A dandy once, he apologized in court about his appearance. 'These are the only clothes I possess,' he told the revolutionary court. Salvation through suffering. A Bahai and a homosexual, an outsider. He asked for a month's reprieve to write his memoirs. Denied. He sought martyrdom.

Letter from father:
'I owe the bank money and have paid 72,000 in interest.'
Letter to father:
'The older I grow the closer I feel towards you. However briefly, there was love between you and mother. Not something to be said lightly.'

It is all a matter of concentration: if you concentrate on wealth, you become a rich man, if on love, a prostitute, if on beauty, a poet, if on god, a saint.

I never sublimated. I lived out every fantasy. Sublimation is turned into work. I became an artist. We are not born with nothing, we are born with a body. I created my own life with my own body; I lived in the inferno and came back to tell what I had seen.

Man plays only when he is truly human and he is truly human only when he is at play.

—Schiller.

'Work cannot be play' is a formulation separating the artist's play from the labour of life. Marx would say that labour humanizes man. The artist labours at his art in extracting what is real from what is apparent, though what is there may not be a 'fact.' Only in the artist's life do work and play intermingle, and alienation ends.

'The gay movement, the women's movement are political. They have nothing to do with the reinvention of love.'
— Octavio Paz

Those who became celebrants (of freedom) have usually been marginal members of their own social group. Even when they were not initially, their taste for liberty tended to make them so, but usually they already were. The recipe seems to be something like this: enough experience, preferably early, of personal security to desensitize the unconscious to the threat of scarcity activated by some kind of stigma, severe enough to loosen the pledge that binds the individual to the group; but not severe enough to get him cast out of the group and thus destroy his security. Nor must the stigma be permitted to become *itself* the basis for a new group membership, for this destroys its effectiveness as a bond-weakener; the individual has taken a new pledge and immediately begins to promote his new group-interests at the expense of his scepticism and inner vision. Being Jewish, being black, being gay—all these used to work wonders in establishing marginality for those who were able to afford it. Today, they avail little; they are just different ways of getting into politics.

—Fridenberg, *Laing*

I have given up obsession.

Rohinton: Through him I have connected with my people. He is a sportsman and a virgin—through him I have connected with my opposite. He is a Scorpio like myself and wears a beard over a small face much as I do. Through him I have connected with myself.

He consistently ignores gossip: this is his virtue. He wishes to fly and cannot. He wishes to marry and cannot. He loved god once; now he has lost him, the Zoroastrian god of the Zoroastrian heaven. He is reading Aurobindo and Hafez.

The 'search' for him is self-conquest: how to conquer one's mental doubts, one's physical limitations. He wages a constant war against luxury, softness and effeminacy by facing the cold and eating plain food. It could be consolidation of the ego merely, but his need of others saves him, love saves him.

I am purifying my life, I am purifying my poem.

'Love's only attraction is 'that it is evil.'

—Baudelaire.

'The Zoroastrian flower ceremony:

An initiate faces a teacher; between them are laid three flowers on the right, for good (good deeds, words and thought), and three on the left, for evil. By the teacher are two flowers, one each for good and evil. The initiate crosses over to the teacher and picks up the evil flower, holds it for long. Then he exchanges it for the flower of truth and reaps seven flowers for experience, strikes a vase filled with the water of feeling nine times for the nine directions and returns to his place. Having known evil and reaped experience, he is ready to return to life.

Met an Iranian Zoroastrian from Kerman. Echoes of Ken again. I was offered a teaching position at his school. I slept in his bed, ate his food. he grilled me before his friends on the issue of my homosexuality. At night in sleep he caught my hand. We shared a shower on the last day of school. We decided to live together the next term. I later learnt he was suspected of being a Savak agent. He had the habits of a spy listening to conversation to form a case. He came to me with a demand for money. I refused. I had to contact the police to recover my books and belongings from him. I had seen him as a spiritual lover prior to my sleeping with him and written him a poem-cycle in the manner of Rumi. The ghost of Ken had been laid to rest finally.

Rohinton left wordlessly, returning all my poems.

Behzad replaced Ken. 'Everything is chance.' He was involved in politics. I gave him his first ever sexual experience with a man. I took responsibility for that. He wished to sleep with my sister. He rejects Freud. He gave me the loyalty he otherwise gave politics. We decided to live together ten years (until his marriage). He brought me a silver-plated ring and recited the first phrases of the wedding rite in Arabic. I wrote a marriage vow: 'It is possible for the beautiful person.' I wished to support his leftist politics financially. He had been jailed for a poem once, he said. He was my opposite: a Taurus to my Scorpio. I decided to take on employment so as to be able to live on earth. I finally understood my rebellion against money as a rebellion against my father; as a perpetuation of my mother's words: 'Money means prostitution.' Behzad came to me out of rebellion seeking freedom and protection and worked through his repressions. I could love a person wholly, bodily and permanently at last. We made each other many promises: the child of the future. 'You are an idealist.' I let him keep his idea of himself. The young boy comes to the experienced man in joy and freedom. He learns and teaches compassion.

In Isfahan I lived in a basement room furnished with a bed on the floor oriental style, over which I threw a Kashmir shawl. My landlady gave me a rug for the floor and her hope chest served as a wardrobe. My poems I kept in a Persian box from Behzad's family.

My landlady's daughter had become estranged from her fiancé and the entire family was enraged in a transatlantic brawl trying to recover stolen gifts and articles from the girl's trousseau.

Letter from Behzad:

Because I did not want to show myself (an inexperienced) person, I told you about Afsaneh . . . I have never met Afsaneh . . . I made up those names. I have suffered much because I lied to you. Every time we had a fight I encountered [*sic*] to hit you because of that. The first body that I have seen in my life was your body. I have never been after your money. I never wanted to use you for myself. I wanted to be with you whatever you are. I am really alone. Please take my hand help me to come out of this prison, the prison that is killing me.

Kurdestan: I took the bus to Sanandaaj. All at once the landscape became magical as were the hills around the Dead Sea or the roads of Cyprus. It was the kind of land one would die for. Summer was at midpoint, rivers full, trees lush, now and then a drongo or a kingfisher in flight. The bus road by the riverbank going onward to its source. Ten checkpoints in an hours' drive. Women and boys were suspected as spies; the guards were hated.

Sanandaaj was bombed completely. Hill cities built much like Rome with sepia-coloured wash on houses. The Medes are said to have reverted to Kurd. Villages lack the barest amenities. Women weave bright red and orange rugs in Tree of Life patterns.

Made love to a Kurd on the night bus.

Letter to Behzad:

Coming upon the knowledge of another person must be deeply shaking.
I only gave my body—I never before took or kept anyone.

YOU ARE THE FIRST ONE WHO STAYED:

I have become an ordinary human being, no longer poet, prostitute or saint . . . Early in our friendship I saw you as a fighter in life and politics. You are without many things. You are extraordinary. So you are my friend.

I am attached to the body, relationships, earth. We are opposites. We complete each other.

You are not divided. You are whole. You can love and befriend the same person.

You taught me discipline: to love without destroying myself every minute, every day. Money is only a means; love is a basis. You are not in prison anymore. You are the dream child; my lost innocence and future success.

I talked to you about the search for god. Man's wanting the absolute, we call 'god'. We lost god after childhood because we lost our childhood loves. To find love again will mean to find god again. But to fail in our human relationships and go to god is a mistake. Men can only love god through men and women. Sex without friendship is a mistake. Everything else besides friendship is from books. Political killing comes from lack of love. The powerful cannot answer the love of the martyrs, nor equal them, so they have killed them. As a young man you understand all this better.

Growing mature you want power; I call you back

to the child that you are. So you say I 'lessened your loyalty.' When the true revolution comes they will probably kill me.

If you are motivated by love then, even when you have money and power, you give it away.

I later learnt that the money meant for politics he had kept himself. Another 'business deal,' too, was probably phoney: he was to have spent that money for study abroad. My contempt for money he had used to his own advantage.

Yet I kept with him as much out of compassion as of need.

The last I tried living with him he talked of terrorism, a romanticized suicide. Marxism has become a superstition of the twentieth-century.

I worked in a boys' school under extreme humiliation and disrespect to support the two of us. His demands for the necessities and comforts of life were unending. I had to break with him.

Behzad wrote me:

Four times
First by fire
Then water, air
Finally earth

Who is this man?
From where? Why?

For whom?
I am not I
Loneliness

is lonely –
Light
More light upon light
Look to the contrary light

I sleep safe as a crook in his arm
Alone

Today is Friday. I can sense time passing with the speed of light. I had been thinking for three hours, leaning to the wall, without knowing where I am [*sic*]. I was dreaming about you, about the days we had together, about the time nobody could separate us. Then I decided to alive [*sic*] the past. The best thing that could help me to remember you were your beautiful letters. So I selected one and copied it for you . . .

I came back after seventeen days. The work is so hard. Ten hours in the desert in cold weather . . .

The poem's second stanza is my translation of impromptu poems he'd recite in bed.

But I could not believe in him any longer.

Boys came to me later but I had ceased to be trusting. My

powers failed me in the very act of love-making.

The effort outlasting the end is one definition of love.

The others have become installed in our hearts, and we call them ourselves. Each person, not being himself to himself or the other, just as the other is not himself to himself or to us, in being another for another neither recognizes himself in the other, nor the other in himself. Hence being at least a double absence, haunted by the ghost of his own murdered self, no wonder modern man is addicted to other persons, and the more addicted, the less satisfied, the more lonely.
—R.D. Laing, *Politics of Experience*

The creative friend, who always has a complete world to bestow. And as the world once dispersed for him, so it comes back to him again, as the evolution of good through evil as the evolution of design from chance.

—Nietzsche

Letter to Freny Bhownagary:
My book turned out to be a kaleidoscope: a few bits of glass reflected endlessly.

The book grows slowly like life by accretions. In installing myself within my book I'm creating my life. If we wish to write the truth then there's only one truth for each man, the truth of his own life. On examining one's unique truth it is not surprising to find that truth touching upon the truth of unique others. Hence the writer who writes for himself is later taken up by others. Only the intellectual brings negative insights to bear upon himself.

My sister left Iran for Bhutan and cut ties with everybody.

Letter from Traute:
>Helmut fell down on his knees and asked me to make him the happiest man there is or else he'd be broken-hearted. I said 'yes' as I don't like a broken-hearted man. I expect my baby in three months.

Tehran School for Foreign Residents: I was to have taught Taiwanese who refused to speak Chinese. Their fathers were third-world frontmen for an American aeronautics company. An American woman ran the school much as a personal fief, reminding me of my American bosses in Heidelberg. Women in business usually learn their office-manner from men.

Letter from sister:
>'David earns $ 13000 yearly and is still broke.'
>I say the monk in him is pining for recognition.

Letter to sister:
You say human nature is beyond you. I understood even the

child I have been seeing lately. Yesterday he came to my city for the first time in a year, since I abandoned him. I took a hotel room and began talking. He finally confessed that he wanted the 'experience of trickery'—a child's greed for experience. 'An act is pure if no turn of reason judges it'—he was pure in trickery! I, for my part, wanted the experience of being 'taken'. There was an unspoken understanding between us. This experience is now lived out, understood, liquidated. His wanting to borrow the amount to repay me touched me. In the morning I said 'Happy Birthday': My travail had finally made him honest; I had taught something.

'Possession—where the possessor possesses nothing.'
—Proust

I planned a dream-trip to Turkey: the dancing dervishes, Istanbul, the Orient Express.

Saw Nagshe-Jehan Square through a morning mist. Isfahan's palace, mosque, marketplace: old friends weeping.

Behzad dissuaded me from going; I stayed though unemployed.

Manfred asked to show my poems in Germany.

Behzad gave me a false address of a business when I asked for the return of my loan. Driving to my hotel during a blackout he killed a cyclist; was jailed a day. I trod incessantly between his home, my hotel and the police station. Via Dolorosa, streets of sorrow, the same streets of sorrow

I walked early mornings on my weekly visits to Isfahan. I would call at his bedroom window, he'd let me into his parents' home.

Now he returned from jail, head shaved, irate and ordered me out of his life. I phoned, wrote letters, sent him Gandhi, the *Gita*, Nietzsche, Castro, Victor Jara.

He warmed to me. Took me to his grandmother's house recently vacated by tenants. In that empty house prevailed an unbearable sense of life being, a prison. An odd eroticism flowered.

We walked through narrow alleys, a covered bazaar and came out again on Naqshe-Jahan. I could not look into his eyes as he wore sun-shades: mosques, minarets reflected therein.

He told me he kept dynamite hidden in his house. It could explode any moment.

He told me he had spent all my money on an automatic revolver. This was the secret for which he had so consistently lied. Loyalty to confused politics had taken precedence over even human considerations.

With my own hand I drowned his anger, the dynamite, in a stream running past his house.

The moon rose, golden, round and full.

He promised to renounce terrorism.

From jail he brought back a painting of Leily and Majnu, in exchange for the gift of his watch.

I will translate his poems and send them to Germany. I write him daily. I promised to work to pay his enormous fine.

What was to be beautiful became a sacrifice.

Unposted letter to Rex:

I cannot tell this to anyone.

My friends here, older American homosexuals in hiding, condemn me. My own friend is a young Persian.

I went for a job interview with a government-run Persian daily. The front page carried a news item of the death by shooting of two boys twenty-four and thirty. I read and reread the story until I fell into a trance-like state compounded of nausea and fear. I hinted to the American secretary that I was gay. I could not work for such people. I did not get the job. Tell me, Rex, there is a place for honesty in a world of prostitutes and lackeys. Absolve me Rex, with your friendship . . .

I wrote to Behzad:

God is nothing but oneself.

Man has to bow to someone: so I bow to you.

If you are too proud you can bow to yourself . . .

At prayer, we bow to the earth because we all live, or really want to live, here.

But he told me he hated himself and considered himself a failure.

To be young means being nobody, so being everybody, being everybody is an act; playing at being womanizer, lover, sodomite, terrorist, fatalist, materialist, criminal, bourgeois. It means the last luxury of remaining passive, of remaining a child. The world impinges upon the child; men impinge on the world. The child's world of irresponsibility. It means being a thing, so as to become a being one stirs up events: chance encounters, dream escapades, real accidents, adventurous holidays, forbidden loves, hard work, prison, heartbreak. It means unspeakable cruelty because the young have no allegiance and are willing to risk everything since they stand to lose nothing not ever having owned anything including their own names. It means unspeakable love because being always outside they embrace with tenderness the lover, the jailed, the underdog, the criminal, the outcast. It means a willingness, an ever-readiness to die, to immolate oneself for a cause larger than oneself. It means being vigilant against the hypocrites who hold on to their shameful lives by the commerce of deceit. It means not accepting anything that is warped, broken, unwhole, unidealistic, and wanting to make, madly, the beautiful on earth. It means deep, dark despair, without words, in a jail without exit because nothing is as it can be. It means not ever feeling guilt at having subdued every relationship, friendship, love, to the mad ideal of blowing up the world to make it new. It means immolating another. The horror of immolating another wakes up the child, the dreaming angel, the slumbering god, and casts him into the hell that most men call their lives.

Only a poet is forever a child.

Letter to Behzad:

You said to me: 'I came to you because I felt myself a failure.'

Do you know where I come from? Let me repeat:

My maternal grandfather was a priest, a man of learning.

My mother was a BA in English forty years ago in India; my paternal grandfather a medical doctor working with the English. (Hence our English surname).

My maternal grandmother came from a family of landowners: The land was given away to Gandhi and later, communists. My paternal grandmother was a high-school graduate, a widow at twenty-five who never remarried.

Her sister married a 'Sir', a man who started India's first bank.

My parents were sexual rebels. So are all my sisters and myself. I say this proudly though I hate people to take low advantage of us. I come from money. But I cancelled 'class'. My father used his power to destroy us.

My mother gave me a love of learning and honesty. From her I learnt patience in suffering and forgiveness. I studied literature to know the *why* of suffering. I want to live an honest life.

Did you see me as a failure? Did you believe society's judgement on me?

(In spiritual life height and depth are one: I am purest at my worst suffering.)

You came to me out of loneliness.

Loneliness touches me. I know it. I want to erase it in another's life.

People are afraid of friendship. They see only obstacles.

I jump over differences of age, nationality, language, sex, education, view of life.

To keep me you lied about your experience. You shouldn't have.

You accepted me. I loved your innocence. I did not 'spoil' you.

'There's no "bad" if there is no mental judgment.' Only, suddenly our friendship opened on to your secret self. I had touched you most deeply and had become your enemy . . .

All the prohibitions of your society came back to you.

Not love but this split aged you.

I wanted you to be free of wrong teaching. Sure I was limited in my help by circumstance; sure, I took from you too. And for whatever you gave at great expense to yourself, I thank you. With you I wanted to write a new story, an impossible story of a man like me and a boy like you who love each other and do not keep other people out. (Love has nothing to do with ownership.)

I did not learn this from books but at great pain from my own life.

In my friendship I have not failed.

You think of yourself as a failure because you are different from others. Love does not satisfy you. Their politics you find repulsive, so you make your own. Your times have failed you: refusing you love, freedom or knowledge. Your people have failed you: refusing you freedom from their old ideas, refusing to see the validity of your new ideas . . .

Your reality as a loving being capable of thinking broadly will find satisfaction in political creation or will turn to crime.

Boy-love is risky; you never know how the boy will turn out.
—*Symposium*

Letter to Behzad:
The prejudiced propagandists write that love between men leads only to pain, hatred, loss, sterility, death. They are men who have failed with women.

(I am thinking of Mailer.) So they kill the homosexual who is trying to live. It is fascism . . . In modern society biology is lost. Men loving men have come to the centre of society (as writers, artists, even politicians in the West) . . . In transitional societies love without responsibility is cannibalism.

Between men the making of a friendship could be the creative act. Why can't we be proud and simple about it?

Until I meet someone willing to be free as me, with me, I will always feel guilt. Guilt spoils everything: living, working, love. Guilt is used as a vice to catch and hold in an unfreeable bond, not eternal love, but a jail. Get rid of guilt, get rid of bondage. This amounts to saying: get rid of your whole childhood influence, your whole rotten society. That is, we are talking politics: MAKE YOUR OWN SOCIETY, where not jealous competition but friendship and sharing are the rule . . .

Fathering ghosts,
I ran from desert to desert
Ejected from the airplane's shadow
My thirst is endless
No fountain can quench it
Friend! Brother! I'll bring you
Corn from the land of Egypt,
Even the corn I do not have,
Egypt, Egypt! I have been thrifty
That I might give to others some day;
Now I am naked, lonely and poor.
God's growing shadow spares me not a moment;
I shall remove this burning choker

And leave you my thirst,
Since I own nothing more.

—D.M. Pettenella (Portuguese)

Letter to Virgil:
The truth of the matter is that people who know nothing of Western culture are teaching it for fancy salaries which buy their European vacations, fashions and homes, which in turn reinforce their right to teach 'Western' culture. Their American wives, smarting from the American humiliation in Iran, intrigue to keep everyone else out. Whores, every one of them. On the other hand Iranians ask me to be their 'secretary'. That I cannot type, take dictation or handle a telephone switchboard does not deter them in the least. Actually, it is very amusing.

Letter to Behzad:

Do not be anxious over my new job possibility in Palestine. It is such small deaths that prepare us to leave, to give up.

I am born in November, end of the year, winter, wisdom, experience, and death before new spring. The star in the sky when I was born was the last of the twelve stars, the two fish, one up, one down. It signifies 'parting' and 'imprisonment'. Love is my prison. Death of love my rebirth. If you will review our months of friendship it was against this death I was always fighting, trying to put it off. 'Life is given for a moment with a friend.' Dishonest people befriend foreigners *because* they leave. You wanted commitment; you were honest. I have great hopes for you . . . When going to a future we must not look back. If we do we'll lose what is ahead of us. I know this myself, from the last time I tried for a job in Palestine.

There is a beautiful Greek story: a poet/god loved his wife so much he went to hell to lead her back out. But he was not to look back at her. He did and lost her . . .

Behzad tells me to write out a long dream of his for him:

He is sleeping in a golden desert with four tall green cypresses standing in a row. An emanation rises from him. He runs after it; it climbs a tree and falls into a well.

He sleeps again in a red sweater and shorts. Breezes blow gently. Four Behzads rise out of his body and go in search of the first lost one. They return with the lost Behzad just in time, because if they hadn't he would be dead.

The child is a spirit wailing for its mother. He comforts it. It becomes an outline etched on his torso: the child's mouth at his genitals, its legs descending to his thighs.

He looks to the moon and as if through a telescope; his naked eye sees a Behzad stumbling on the moon.

CUT

He is stumbling in Europe. I come with mounted escorts,

pick him up and take him to a skyscraper. It takes half an hour by elevator to ascend to the top of the building where my offices are. Servants bow deferentially and bring coffee. I strip and show a vagina. Behzad is shy but I remain naked before servants, sip coffee. I ask him if he needs money. He narrates the story of his automobile accident. I write out a check so that he can pay up his fines in Iran and return.

When he returns from Iran it is still coffee time for me!
CUT
Iran: The picture of Khomeiny that had been put up where the Shah's statue was, has now been pulled down. I am rushed to hospital in an ambulance and Behzad runs to my aid. Ten doctors work on my body and he thinks I'm out of danger.

The next night he dreamed of a classic vampire-woman.

From a letter to elder sister:

America's is a leprosy with fair hair, blue eyes, and white skin. Some Americans are insidious, behind their 'liberal' masks they are lepers; other blue-eyed all-American boys like David are their *victims* without knowing it . . .

How can you ask me to change? (If being gay is what you want me to change.) It suits sisters without marital loyalties to have fag-brothers just as it delights mothers without husbands . . . It suited you to literally mould me in your image.

I was burnt by you in Chicago (Paul telling me to put down ten cents for a phone call), in Israel ($30 short), in Germany (Paul screaming in the streets for my stereo you practically gifted David when I was penniless); you withheld mail from me (the Vermont Buddhists' letter to me was never forwarded); you sent my diplomas to family in India who withheld them for a year; you took gifts from me, including gold gifted to me in my poorest days and when sending help sent driblets ($150 during the Iranian Revolution) and now $200 ('You can repay me from your substantial Israel salary'). I charged you with duties or asked you favours because of my trust in you, which you abused . . .

Why do I write you? Because by living in America you made a decision I dared not make (had the good sense not to make) and for the disadvantages of which I sympathize with you. I write you because you are, in a sense, familyless: husband or childless; even your own family does not write you . . .

Life is more than rose bowers, lily ponds, cut glass, gardens planted with flowers named A to D, traffic tickets, cars, apartments, houses, European trips, running away from father, adopting and ruling over cats, orphaned girls, emotionally stunted men or fag-brothers. Life is pain and life's work is alleviating that pain in others. If you can't help, at least, don't hurt.

Letter to father:
You write: 'You live your life. So why shouldn't I live mine?' This in response for my asking news from you. What I hear you saying to me is: 'You are the mistake of my past and I do not want to meet up with it.' To that extent your envision is a confession of guilt, a bearing up of your responsibility and to that extent I am freed. Illness has ceased to be an absurd fate and has become instead a generalized possibility for existence.

Second letter to sister:
I am so ashamed of having hurt you. I want to tell you why I did it.

I hate America: I'll never return to live there. This much is certain. You became a symbolic 'America' for me to slay.

I am a poet obsessed with experience—knowing it if for nothing other than the fulfilment of describing it, even the experience of failure. (Especially the latter in a success-crazed world.) I understand as I say in a poem: 'What has no resale value cannot be funded.' At the same poem's end I talk about the 'stone ripening to cherry 2700 years in Fukien (a press report)'. I want bankers to understand this. No interest can be paid by a poet on the time of his maturing. (Or, for that matter by any man.) It is as if society has gambled with the poet's life and must pay him.

That payment is approval: 'You are a poet. Carry on.' Poems come only from the lived, killed, life. You always approved of the end product but not the process that made it. I know approval to be creative: my approval made a small-town 'adulteress' into a 'poet'.

Sibling rivalry is planted, nurtured and made to fructify in decadent society. ('Of course America is great. It is a result of decadence.'—Jorge Luis Borges.) It is planted by neurotic parents and its fruit is social success. It kills personal relationships in the family and creates neurotics venting themselves on anyone at random. As we mature we learn to mask envy as solicitude. Both of us do it to each other—examples are legion. (We just have to accept our own dark hearts and make them light over and over.)

Being a very jealous person I cope with jealousy by not competing. In ten years of bar-going I never competed actively for a lover; in ten years of job-searching I never competed actively for a job against a friend. I could not hurt anybody because of a fine conscience, because of a weakness in me that cannot hurt others, nor face up to the jealousy in my own heart. I took failure upon my head rather than facing up to the need to hurt other animals in the jungle. (My overnight vegetarianism that greyed me prematurely was actually only an extreme symptom of this disease.) A very jealous competitor told me: 'In the modern sense of an old-fashioned word you are a saint.'

I had earned my badge. 'You are a failure in your own eyes,' you tell me. No, I chose purposely a difficult path which few start upon, the path of 'saint' or 'poet' which by definition includes 'sinner' and 'destroyer'.

Carmela writes, 'Gays live in society without ending up in poorhouses.' The disease is not being gay; the disease is poetry. ('I want to be a debauch when I live, and when I die I want to be revered as a saint.'—Fath Ali Shah Qu'ajar.) Just being gay is punishable with death in an Islamic society. Some gays succeed by acting straight—a game not worth the candle to me. Virgil respects me: 'You did it in your life. You were mad enough.'

This 'madness', 'neuroticism', dismissed contemptuously by father, mocked gently by Carmela, railed against and pitied alternately by you, is the very creative germ from which masochism ends and creation begins. I know myself from failure in love. We are trying CHANGE: from the destructive to the creative.

Your judgements, even the mildest, most correct or most honest ones hurt me as you have become the parent (mother dead, father abandoned).

Monetary help is a way of saying, 'I am with you.' (Hence, I accepted your share of mother's estate and never claimed it—I'll return it to you in all justice.)

We have a touching need for each other. Really, there is no need to make a melodramatic hell out of this need.

A thief makes off with $13,000 from Behzad's father. Behzad wishes he were the thief. I see no hope for him.

My sister writes me:
> I had the weirdest dream about you. You were leaving and the authorities confiscated all your books on grounds they were a 'national heritage' and locked them up in museums. So I decided to go rescue them for you. I would know which were yours because all had red leather binding. I borrowed a red sports car to camouflage the red books and went running around a strange museum to get you back your writings.

I started typing up all my manuscripts and shipping them out one by one.

Letter to sister:
> The dream presents a catch-22 situation much like my life. If I'm a 'national heritage' (a poet) people feel I need to be rescued, however once I'm rescued I am no longer a poet.

Both Freud, in emphasizing early childhood, and Marx, in emphasizing class, stress the effect of environment upon man. Only one thing transcends environment and that is the imagination.

'Communism comes through the heart. And the heart

belongs to the realm of poetry.'—Voznesensky, Russian poet.

When the ancient Persians or Hindus said 'sacrifice', they meant 'creation'. Creation means a birth: of a musical being. Music, poetry are most akin to the mystic states.

'A work of art, like carnal love, does not allow a fall into the mundane as long as it lasts.'

Letter from Pritish Nandy, Indian poet:
> Some of your poems are very powerful. I like them very much. It is time these poems saw print.

The lyric poem like life comes from nothing and goes into nothing. Thirty years: childhood, inferno, emergent living. The circle is yet incomplete.

Tehran–Isfahan
1979–1980

Circle of Hell
Palestine, Palestine

Prologue

This work is rewritten; the original lost, stolen or simply destroyed by a hater. Works of love also inspire hate.

Reiynaldo Arenas, a gay writer in Castro's Gulag rewrote his autobiography four times. Each time the prison guards destroyed it by fire the work arose, phoenix-like, from the same fires.

Today Castro is gone; his brother Raul, rumoured to be gay by Genet, has legalised gay unions in Cuba.

In Israel now gays march in the streets accompanied by a police escort for protection against their religious Right: 1000 policemen for 500 gays; each gay with two smart 'straight' men to protect him!

Changed India, too: my autobiography will be printed.

3.00 a.m
1 April 2008

I
Nablus
1982, Tehran

My game in Iran had played out; my love unspooled. What was to have been delight became a sacrifice. Time to leave!

Istanbul: A teaching offer in Istanbul for $100 monthly. Can I subsist merely on a vision of those golden domes? I chose Jerusalem. A year-long wait in the Tehran Poorhouse before joining.

The Revolutionary Guards at Meherabad Airport insulted me as I left:

—English teacher? We don't need any!

I sat down in my plane-seat and wept as if something had broken within me.

They went through my bags, my papers.

—What is this paper, paper! Show us your hidden gold!

I had carried a 20-rial note as a souvenir of that pre-revolutionary Iran, before Iran fell into the hands of goons.

Nablus

Once a chance meeting with Ayatollah Beheshti at seven in the morning at Tehran's Interior Ministry. He was huge; totally unprotected. He turned around like a lumbering elephant and gave me a sharp look as if memorising the features of a future assassin. The Left bombed him out of existence soon.

Rashda Masri came to the Ben Gurion Airport, Tel Aviv to greet me. Pink dress, pink scarf on head, not a day older than fifty.

'If you're a Communist we can't keep you'!
—I'm not a Communist!
'If you're a homosexual, ditto!'
—I'm not a homosexual.
My perjury had begun.

Palestine rose out of the bottom of the prehistoric sea, Tethys. It has hillocks and valleys, deserts and sudden rivulets forming valleys (or wadis i.e. water gullies). The Jordan flows into the Dead Sea. There are water wars between nations in the area now. The Mediterranean is hugged by the Gaza coast. These are Cretans (sea peoples of Ramses' inscription) who settled here. The Phoenicians were seafaring and known for the purple dye made from molluscs. Mt Lebanon's slopes were covered by cedars out of which the Temple was fashioned. The chalky sub-soil over laterite limestone allows the olive to spread its roots in shallow soil and grow hundreds of years. Grapes, oranges, figs and almonds are native to Palestine. Find two almonds in a shell they say and you'll find love. Palestinians live on mountain tops and work the fertile valleys. Now Israel builds on peaks to shoot into a restive town below. At the narrowest Israel is only 17 km wide. This is the corridor between Gaza and the West Bank. Choke this chicken neck and you bifurcate north Israel from the south. In Dimona (Negev) Cochin Jews laboured in cotton.

The driver lost his way to Nablus. We arrived by moonlight to a hulking dark hillock. 'Nablus!' said Rashda.

'You're Blake! You can hear angels singing in trees!'

—Indeed, I did!

The next morning on my way to campus a boy caught up with me. Could it be a new love? No! He was looking for recruits for the PFLP. Rashda hated them. The hatred was mutual.

Rashda's uncle had started the school with his gay friend, the late poet Ibrahim Touqan—Fadwa's brother—who still lived downhill at one of the first bends in the road where I too was put up.

Nablus
is a woman
weeping for a lover
She treads stones
on bare feet

Nablus

At the purple sun-set hour
she weeps . . .

'Such a sad poem!' Rashda said. 'I hope everyone will say you teach well!'

'You must love' said Rumi. 'If you're married, love your family. If not, love a friend!'

This was maliciously reported to Rashda as my espousing gay causes. I was merely peeking out of the closet!

A fellow teacher of Shakespeare once herded his uncle's sheep on the hill pasture of Palestine. He had no shoes on his feet. Now he'd returned from Oxford with a thesis on Cleopatra! He espoused the Palestinian cause. Everyone espoused the Palestinian cause. As long as it benefited them. Politics and oil money.

Another invited me to Salfit. I declined. I did not wish to cause a commotion in a Palestinian village. I thought him to be a bisexual. He was a Casanova. Indeed, in a year's time he lost his job (as I did) for soliciting students.

Strikes, sit-downs at school. Against the Israelis. Rashda too would strike. Against the striking students. For not knowing their conjugations. I sat at sit-ins with the PFLP students, George Habash's party. The Democrats of Nayef Hawatmeh tried to woo me, unsuccessfully. I had lost my heart to Nabil of the PFLP. He was second-in-command. Their leader was a thick fellah.

Nabil's hair shone in the sun. It fell in curls. His head was well-oiled. With olive oil. Olive oil was the liquid gold of Palestine. When the young revolutionaries smoked too much their choked, blackened lungs were relieved of phlegm by drinking a glass of olive oil, neat! Then back to a six-pack day. I called Nabil, 'Lancelot.' That he was to become: A ladies' man. That was what the revolution taught our boys, the Moslems would grumble. Guards in Jewish jails probably solicited Nabil. He probably knew gay sex but I saw him as virginal.

He took me home to his mother. 'He slept with me thirteen years when his father was away in the coal-mines of Ruhr!'

'Welcome! Ahlen-Wasalen!' was all the father muttered, over and over. No language!

'I love you most, after my mother!' Nabil said to me.

He took me to the village cemetery. A small plot on a wind-swept slope.

Bury me here!

—'No, go home to your people!' said Nabil.

A martyrs' cemetery. Martyrs of love.

I was so touched by the simplicity, the poverty, the sincerity. I gave away my first salary to the PFLP.

—You're mad! said Rashda.

She was right. They drank, smoked, womanised, plotted revolution, eight long years of Occupation. 'The Israelis will come to India too', said Nabil. Indeed they did, to Sri Lanka.

'Our fathers too fought. In the 1930s. They were defeated. Kicked by the hooves of British Officers' horses in Mandate Palestine,' the Poet informed me.

I called him the Fat Poet. With a bandaged head, from a stone-throwing demonstration, he looked like Apollinaire, trepanned. He wore a Moroccan cape for dramatic effect. I tried on the cape. I waddled in it. But he was a bad poet. And dishonest, too.

—'Why fat? Just Poet, would do!' he'd admonish me.

He took me to Jenin. His brother, prize-student of Jenin High School (now the University of Palestine, Jenin) knew immediately I was gay and wished me to give him some experience. I do not attack my hosts' children. That night, during a power cut (the patriotic village had disconnected itself from the Israel power grid and Israel wouldn't allow a link-up with Jordan) they all huddled under the magic Moroccan cape. They all huddled, cuddled and giggled. I saw the family's genius with his sister. They bundled and giggled. The girl giggled, the boy giggled, the father too giggled. A peasant attitude to the body. I sat sourly next to the sweaty Fat Poet who stank.

Power cuts can be fun. They can be tragic too. The newspapers reported a mother lacing her bride-to-be daughter's school sandwich in the dark at dawn with rat-poison, thinking it to be black pepper. The high school girl merrily ate it: her last sandwich as a carefree lass. She was brought home from school, dead. A scene of rejoicing became a scene of mourning. Palestinians are used to that.

Someone picked up a stone to throw across the picket of burning tyres. The Israeli ace-shooter shot him in the arse. Hip bone shattered. Heroism mattered. In hospital the hero shrieked for his mom! She ran to his bedside. I was there: with rabbit and 'mlukhiya' (chard) cooked by my revolutionaries at home. One more hero was disappointed. Wailing like a child in pain. I caused a sensation at the hospital in my white kurta-pyjama. Florence Nightingale from India with a soup tureen held in outstretched arms! The nurses came to look. Everyone wanted to know my exact relations with the hero.

At another rally a seventeen-year-old picked me up and took me to his mother and elder brother, twenty-six, a high school math teacher. The mother, a busty woman in Western attire, a widow, looked like an Arab Shelley Winters. The elder son, a Communist, almost brainwashed his mother into becoming an atheist. She was repenting when we met. The Party would not let the young believe in God or love. They took the youth away from the struggle. An elaborate rigmarole involving a lit match was used to prove that like the heat and light of an extinguished matchstick neither God nor love existed! I'd say you feel the heat but not see it: God and love are just like that. But who's listening to me, in Palestine! At night they separated me from the boy and asked me to sleep with the elder brother. I held out all night but couldn't resist him by dawn. He feigned sleep, opened an eye at orgasm and promptly went back under his blanket. The next night I was given the couch in the hall. I left the home in rain; the garden hung with pomelos as big as lanterns. I remembered Heine's 'Home-Coming': the eternally wandering Jew hoping to come home some day.

'My son is not beautiful, your eyes are beautiful,' a cobbler had said to me in Iran when I praised his son's beauty. Nablus has its share of cobblers. I fell in love with the son of one. 'Take him! Take him!' the father said. They always said that. Ten children to a family: to change the demography of Israel. A political act. Every mother a revolutionary birthing future revolutionaries. (Hence the Naga cannibals in India's north-east once ate enemy women: They birth future enemies!) Too many mouths to feed! Yes, hands for labour too. But not enough labour in the cities. Unemployment, listlessness. Take him! He tried to rape me in the maze of alleys in the Old City.

Stolen
Stolen fruits are always sweeter
Stolen kisses much completer
Stolen looks are good in chapels
Stolen, stolen be your apples.
—Anon. (Old English Rhyme)

On winter days boys and girls would saunter up and down

the college quadrangle: boys with boys, girls with girls. But the boys would go in one direction, the girls in the other. It was like Dante's Florence after Sunday churchgoing. Same-sex love flourished. A male music teacher took my hand to walk against his girl's direction. I pummelled his palm for good measure. She sent word he was not to be seen with me. We hid in the Music Room. He would play an instrument; I, write. Teachers, mostly men, peered in at the shut window. He would play a plaintive flute melody till tears welled in my eyes. He'd feel powerful; I, helpless. I'd quarrel with him then. 'O, Dawood,' he'd say helplessly. I'd feel some triumph then. 'Dawood' is Arabic for David, the type for male friendship in youth and prophecy in age. We ended up in bed. We made love thrice in one night. I had to banish him to the living room where other guests, students, slept. They reported us to the Party. The party parted us. I showed up at school beardless. It was a scandal. When I visited his home in the neighbouring town he played loudly a tape of Koranic verses (to cast out the devil) and ordered me out of his life. We never talked again. After four years of ogling his sweetheart and amassing a bride-price ('mehr'), they married. When I left town after a year, we chanced upon each other on the high street. He kissed me goodbye.

Bassem would be another boy who'd accost me at sunning-time in the piazza. He'd brush his body against mine and get a thrill. I visited his student room but he was always at prayer.

Nablus

When he visited me, flushed hot with anticipation, I gave him a chaste kiss and sent him away. Bassem remembered me as the chaste Yusuf. When they denounced me in the mosque, Bassem stood up for me. His wife later wickedly said that it was I who was keen on Bassem, that Bassem was never keen on me. It was not that the bird was keen on Prometheus but that Prometheus was keen on the bird. Bassem, forty now, appears on BBC to defend Palestinian Human Rights. I remember the full-lipped boy with slim waist and an ample endowment with a pang.

When Israel invaded Lebanon, school shut down. Everyone got tired chasing everyone else. They stayed home plotting Revolution. I strayed into the PFLP den. The head honcho, an Israel-prison graduate, hence older, was getting his body massaged by his younger minions. I volunteered to massage him. We were not alone and he had to keep up his image among his protégés, so he wouldn't succumb to my wiles. I was soon banned. Called an Israeli spy. When I protested I did not understand their language they said even a deaf mute outsider couldn't attend their party proceedings. 'What party do you belong to?' the Lahore jail inmates asked the poet Faiz's friends proceeding to his cell with a birthday cake.

—'The birthday party!' they exclaimed.

I hated Head Honcho and even rejoiced when the Israelis put him behind bars in preventive detention without a trial for eighteen days. But when my boy, Nabil, went to jail I pretended to be a Palestinian, wore an Arafat 'Kefiyeh', wept, spent sleepless nights, publicly declaimed my poems declaring love for the Leftist martyrs and become the laughing stock of the Islamists.

Everyone wrote poetry. Everyone publicly declaimed. A woman teacher, divorced, leftish, spoke passionately about Palestine. She could see I was a fox in the chicken coop. Our hatred was mutual. To her I was always 'the foreigner'. The Islamists wickedly put it out that her family beat her up at home for talking freedom abroad.

'Revolution is not a tea-party'—Mao.

The Arab market (souq): Men with men drinking tea (chai), playing backgammon, fidgeting with worry-beads (tasbiha), calling out to each other with sweet endearments, 'ya habibi' (my darling) being very commonly used. Workless, worthless people awaiting to push Israel into the sea. Breakfast was in the souq : Chickpeas (hummus) or bean soup (fool) with flatbread (khobs). Meat and potatoes were staples at lunch. Feasts consisted of roasted lamb in rice (mansaf) eaten communally from one vast platter. Ramadan fasts in the heat caused kidney failure. Gluttony led to fat, indolence. I thought the society to be homoerotic. I was wrong. The Arabs are homosocial, men with men until night, which was reserved for wives. They went at dawn to the mosque like newly washed lambs. As far the directionless young, they went into the mouth of

Israeli fire, lambs to slaughter. If angered they'd say: 'Talhas teesi' (lick my ass).

I tired of the Revolution. I longed for the sea. 'Donkey-Dick', for that's what everyone called him because of his big dong visible under his trousers, drove six Arabs in a 'service' taxi to the Israeli sea at Netanya. It seemed for the moment that Israel had pushed Arabs into the sea instead of the other way round as the PLO slogan then claimed.

At leisure at the taxi-stand in the Nablus market 'Donkey-Dick' would be polishing his car with master strokes; stroking his dick for future clientel. He'd solicit me but I'd avoid him. Pay my fare by dropping the shekels into his wide open palm and leave for the beach. I soon ended up on the gay, nude beach.

I stumbled upon Priscilla of the Desert. S/he hadn't been reincarnated yet on Hollywood celluloid. But here was the living type. If only I knew! Thinking him to be an Adonis I was soon tossed up into his hot embraces, enjoying his kisses. But this was Venus with a penis. S/he turned and slept on her stomach. I slipped manfully into her manhole. Coming took some doing for lack of friction. I persisted a full half hour under the desert sun only to have my performance applauded by a group of gay voyeurs on a sand-bluff above us!

I'd hide my belongings under a rock and go swimming: no watches, wallets, rings and things on the beach. The beachcomber was a thief: the Russian immigrant as scavenger. I was left clothesless. Clad in swimming trunks I asked the Israeli fairies for help. They quizzed me. About my politics. Hot, hungry and literally naked I stuck to my guns. Jews were OK Zionists were not. Wasn't every Jew a Zionist in Zion? Walk naked to Nablus, they commanded! Donkey-Dick came to my rescue. He literally gave me the shirt off his back and a free ride. I still wouldn't relent. Ingrate that I was, I brought out from my almirah my last shekels on reaching home and dropped them into his ample, expectant palms. But Donkey-Dick had redeemed himself. Not so the mosque.

On my next foray to the beach I was followed by a spy: a thin, big-dicked Arab with dirty teeth and a huge erection. Feeling shy, my spy hung his underwear on his peg as if it were a coat hanger. I laughed then. But he reported everything to the mosque. And I had as good as lost my job.

But sympathy swung my way soon. Another foray, another misadventure. At the Israeli checkpoints they pulled the Arab workers out of the bus, I along with them. They were kicked, punched, humiliated. I thought I was safe until they chanced upon my newly bought copy of *Arafat* published in London, sold only in Israel, not in the Occupied Territories. 'Motherfucker!' said the young soldier to me landing a stinging slap on my left ear. I smarted from the pain and the humiliation. 'What the fuck!' I involuntarily protested. He kicked my left shin, dragged me out of the drill line and took me to his sergeant lounging with a beer under tamarisk trees. 'Forgive my men. They are hot and harassed. His blood boiled seeing enemy Arafat's photo on your book jacket . . . You don't have a residence permit. (Israel never gave one to foreigners working on the West Bank.) You'll have to come to the police station!'

Next day was Shabbat. 'Policeman says you'll have to stay in the lock-up overnight and be produced in court on Sunday morning,' said the woman officer, jiggling her breasts in my face to mock the fairy that she had apprehended me to be. She was definitely her officer's moll.

'Can I go to prison with the women?' I pleaded fearing gay rape.

—'The women will rape you the minute you enter,' laughed the officer.

My guardian angels spoke to me:

—'Lie! Lie all you can, Hoshang, and get out of here.'

'Excuse me!' I started. 'I know the Governor of the West Bank, an Arabic Professor at Hebrew University. My college president and I had 'kunafeh' (a sticky Arab sweet) with him when he visited Nablus. It was on TV!'

Officer: 'You were on TV!'

—'No, I wasn't but my college president was. I must've been somewhere in the background!'

—LET HIM GO!

I was a hero to the PLO. The mosque, as usual, mocked. I read up on Islam and the Arabs. But I could not read up on

Arafat. It was a forbidden book in the forbidden territory; forbidden to all, that is, except the Zionists. Greater Israel! Arabs had to be sacrificed to it.

Jordan was no better. If anyone spoke against the King he was simply pushed off a cliff into the wilderness beneath. A mad Arab killed 'mad' King Abdullah at Friday prayers at Al-Aqsa. The bullet grazed the boy Hussein's medal on his chest. Hussain, soon to be King had become a hero already. 'It was all a CIA plot,' said my Arab students.

Truth shifts like a mirage in the desert. Depends on who is telling the story. The vanquished never write history, the victors do. Israel was lost the day they conquered the West Bank (1976). The Kibbutzim dream vanished with cheap Arab labour. Israel turned capitalist and later colonialist. All the pass laws of the British occupiers were kept intact on the West Bank.

A loyalty oath. The beautiful 'civilian' governor of the West Bank, an academic, thought up a plan to make West Bank intellectuals answerable to Israel. (Actually there is no 'civilian' Israeli. Every Arab citizen between sixteen and sixty enlists in the Army. This is true of women and gays, as well.) It was decided no one will sign up; Israel will expel foreign faculty refusing to fall in line with it but the PLO will reward them with a bonus totalling the year's salary. I was wilfully kept in the dark. I was given a paper in Arabic and Hebrew. The same officer who had once before questioned me told me in broken English: 'Say you don't like the PLO!'

—Wallahi! I don't! I protested. (I detested Arafat for his dictatorship.)

—Then sign here.

I signed.

My fate was sealed.

'Traitor!' No one would talk to me. From the mosque they emptied a basket of used toilet paper on my head as I passed under their window. A child threw a stone at me which barely missed me, landing at my feet. Police bundled off the Arab teachers who'd refused to sign on back to the Trans-Jordanian Eastern bank of the river. One made as if to slap me but was restrained by others. I left for India and my contract was torn up by Rashda Masri.

My sister came to my rescue: 'How can you be a traitor to Palestine? You're not even Palestinian!'

'What you want is freedom', she added.

Besides the boys, I had other good friends in Palestine. Crissie and Steve were Mennonite volunteers. As kids they could not smoke, drink, curse nor fornicate. On a date they'd rub each other standing up on the dance floor in Indiana because 'Dancing is not allowed!' They gave me food and friendship. I suspected the husband was bisexual: he had a Black Arab lover ('a mystical friendship') from their sports club from a previous stint (before his marriage) in Jerusalem. The wife saw through my masochism: 'Because you can't get a screw out of these puritanical Arab boys you let the Israeli authorities screw you. You want to be screwed,' she said to me angrily at seeing me hurt myself.

Kamel Al-Muganni, the Arab painter of Palestine, was another friend. His mother sold her gold bangles and sent him to Cairo Art School when the father was powerless to wrest his land back from the Israelis at Lod, where Ben Gurion Airport now stands. Instead, he was pressed into the chain gang laying the airport tarmac. An older woman in Egypt taught him sex and love. He worshipped his mother. She was a sprightly woman, though heavy of build, with a twinkle in her blue eyes. Swaddled in white muslin she seemed to waft in the hot afternoon haze like a Madonna. Kamel often asked her to sit for his portraits of Gaza women. 'He wants to sell me,' she'd joke when those portraits found buyers. He introduced me to his wife and children. The wife cooked me fish from Gaza. The children were amused by my drama. Little Ramzi, the middle child, was my favourite. The littlest one was chubby but fell ill often. The painter would spend sleepless nights. 'Every child suffers an occasional fever!' his wife would try to pacify him. He would sketch me as I ranted and raved alternately at the PLO and the Israelis. Next day his sketch of me would morph into an Israeli face in his Goyaesque crowd-scenes of the Revolution! But he broke our friendship the day I signed Israeli's loyalty oath. Kamel was loyal to the PLO though he left politics for art. He hated other Arabs, 'We're from Crete,' he'd say, meaning 'the sea-peoples' conquered by Ramses II.

Kamel used women's embroidery patterns in his paints. This was 'turath' (tradition). A way of keeping old Palestine alive. Another tradition was the 'Dabki' dance performed at harvest by men.

Another friend Hani, a librarian, walked out of my birthday celebrations the minute he knew I kept cordial relations with my boss, Rashda. He was a fellah, and Rashda of the haute-bourgeoisie, a class enemy. Politics had the Arabs divided; occupation bred paranoia. Hani's mad mother was walled up in a room and they fed her food through a hole in the wall. They would not let the father remarry because they wished to keep the property themselves, away from any future heirs. In spite of cruelty to the mad and to animals the East is very kind to its children.

Mme Abdul-Hadi was a patron of Mughni's revolutionary art. I once stole into an Abul-Hadi orchard and stole an orange. 'You are a thief!' intoned Mme. Hadi in mock-tones of accusation.

Fadwa Touqan, my sequestered neighbour, I met once in the marketplace. She took off her glove to shake hands with me. Hers is the softest hand I've ever touched. After the Occupation she intoned a pious hope that just as the West Bank had made peace with the British they would also eventually accommodate the Israeli settlers. This infuriated the radicals, she was branded an accomplice of

Israel, and forced into self-imposed exile. Her voice was silenced. Palestine was the poorer for it because of the loss of the pained poems she had once written lamenting Palestine's fate as a virginal bride-to-be who'd lost her man on her wedding day. She never married and lived with her gay brother until he predeceased her. I lament never having known Fadwa but she lives for me in her poems.

My last friend in Nablus was a student from Til, a village famed for its figs which went all over the Roman Empire. Cleopatra's basket of figs came from Til! He brought me two fresh figs from his tree each morning, dripping with sap. He played volleyball and had an athletic body. I desired him. 'Rishi!' 'Samaki!' 'My feather!' 'My fish!' the boys would exhort the players. He took me home and offered me his elder brother, a labourer in Israel, thick as a brick, who sent my friend to school. They fed me sparrows and the famished youngest girl in the family hungrily eyed my repast as I ate. I saw his class notes and each time I mentioned the word 'sex' in my lecture the notes had a dash or a blank space! He was so modest. We slept separately that night. When I left for India I left some money with the school so that he could complete his education. I pined for him for many moons and then I forgot him: my moon seen from behind my arms, leafless, like a fig tree's.

I had some noble Communist students. One, a girl, had placed a bomb in a women's toilet at Hebrew University when only eight. She had come out at eighteen, in a prisoners swap after ten years in jail. She was rumoured to have become gay in prison. After marriage she discarded jeans and dressed in more feminine skirts. Another, a man of thirty, told me a copy of Picasso's 'Guernica' had kept him sane in jail for five years.

A young woman dentist who had studied in Pakistan liked people from the subcontinent. I lent her 100 dinars which she paid back ten dinars at a time over ten months. But she was honest. The artist Kamel had set up an assignation with her, he told me, and she arrived with a schoolteacher known to both of them! He was left red-faced. She too got married and all that talk about being married to Palestine evaporated.

'And the dogs go on with their doggy lives.'

—Auden

A volleyball player was brought home to me by my students. He had a manic habit of going through his host's house like a whirlwind opening every cupboard, drawer and trunk. I thought he looked sex-starved and was looking for pornography. May be the children had set him up to finding some evidence incriminating me as a gay. That condom, or this lube tube! Nothing was found. He ran about in silk boxer shorts and just as easily slipped out of them. He could have been Samson from Gaza: The brute as lover.

Sami was my 'minder' from the Party. I realise this only now. He was there when I slept with the music teacher. He was also present in the Israeli Traffic Court where I had taken a rash Arab taxi-driver for negligent driving. He made me and the errant driver make peace with a handshake. The school never forgave me for this. Sami had a girlfriend, Nabila, but she was his 'beard'. He was gay and known to haunt the gay garden in Jewish Jerusalem looking to fellate his tormentors. My informant from the mosque he roughed up badly. He took me to his native Gaza. Everyone was impressed with my simplicity calling me 'Gandhi'! Except an uncle who saw through my mask and banned me from the wedding feast.

I have four big notebooks on my year in Nablus. Those books I had to hide at friends' houses from the prying eyes of both Palestinians and Israelis. Freny in Paris preserved all my poems.

II

Jerusalem (1983–84)

Across the river
Is a boy
With a bum like a peach
Too bad I cannot swim

—British Army Marching Song

One soldier dead
One cock and two balls gone waste, I say
Two soldiers dead
Two cocks and four balls wasted
Three: Three cocks and six balls…
(And so on…)

—An Israeli Gay Poet

Israel is a melting pot. 'O Jerusalem, if I forget thee / Let my right hand forget my cunning.' The British evenly divided Palestine; the Arabs went to war and lost everything. Deir Yasin, a massacred Arab village, now is an Israeli joggers park. No trace of Arabs. In the streets the South American,

Russian, Ethiopian Falasha, European jostles for space with the Orthodox Jew. The Orthodox believe this is only an Earthly Garden. They await a Celestial Jerusalem. They, like Arabs, wish to annihilate this modern-day Sodom. Men solicited me in the street: the Italian superstitiously touched his holy trinity when I cast an evil eye on it; the South American opened his right eye with his right forefinger in a gesture meaning 'Come, fuck me'. There are more Jews in New York than here and those here all have dual passports. Every Israeli village has an Arab history, which in turn hides an Old Testament history. The Zionists were overjoyed when they got the Holy Land instead of Kenya to settle displaced European Jewry. I did see an old Jew in a bus hiding his Nazi number tattoo on his forearm that ran into thousands. When I became hysterical at Bertolucci's *1900* depicting Fascist slaughter of Jewish kids, an old Jew hushed me up. The Hebrew University on Mt Scopus and the Kiryat Arba settlement are defences.

Walter Benjamin discussing Paul Klee's painting of the Jewish Angel of History says that the angel flies and blows an apocalyptic trumpet (remember, the walls of Jericho fell!) but s/he looks backwards as she flies ahead. Benjamin explains that this double vision of a future/past had been the fate and history of all Jewry at all times. Even Martin Buber, for all his Jewish humanism lived in a Jerusalem home stolen from Arabs. When I told Palestinians I too am homeless they tittered.

Jerusalem

'Home is a place in the heart/Without it you cannot build/with stone.'

—Brodsky

Jerusalem is an open city. One could move between Arab East Jerusalem and Israeli suburbs to the West. In between lay the old Arab cemetery used by both Arabs and Israelis as a gay garden. It was a meeting point of desire between victim and victimiser and the roles were easily reversed in acts of gay sex performed under the public gaze.

Then, we could go between and between as Shakespeare's Pandarus would say in *Troilus and Cressida*. I lived at the edge of West Jerusalem on Naomi Street overlooking the Valley of Thieves, the same where Ruth stood 'amid the alien corn' remembering home. The Arab village of Abu Dis lay across the valley where I worked. Now Abu Dis is separated by the Jewish Claw which they infamously also call the Wall. Conversely, Abu Dis Science College calls itself the National University of Palestine where Arafat's erstwhile Foreign Minister is University President. In my day Zohair Karmi, BSc (Imperial College, London) had hired me. He spoke softly and carried a big stick. He unsuccessfully asked me to do likewise.

The Dead Sea: I visited with Imad. I had made love to Imad when I stayed one night at his place, with his father already stirring in the next room preparing for dawn's Fajr prayers. The Dead Sea is the site of ancient Sodom. God sent a beautiful angel to the Sodomites to warn them of impending destruction unless they changed their wicked ways. The Sodomites seduced the angel instead. Sodom was destroyed. Sown with salt. Lot's wife looking back at her home became a pillar of salt.

Eilat on the Red Sea, Aqaba on the other side where Lawrence of Arabia met Faisal. The seeds of today's conflicts sown deep in history.

At the submarine sea life museum we saw strange sea creatures: reefs, anemones, sea cucumbers. Also, creatures of the dark, luminescent themselves, who lived by their own lights and could brook no daylight, so deep down under did they live that indeed no light shone there. A predator, ugly, black tentacled: A threat to all other life forms.

Imad was initiated into sex by a crippled priest of the Greek Orthodox Church. His football coach had warned him: 'Those who do, will be done one day.' Imad remembered this prophecy when in bed with me. He was thin, tall and wiry but hung like a horse. To put an end to his male chauvinism I kept him in bed one day, all day at Eilat until he was exhausted and begged for mercy.

At the graveyard people made love athwart graves. Love and Death.

Taraboom di-day
I'm sitting on a tomb

di-day
Tara-boom!

I chanced upon Sabtai, Ran's married neighbour, there. He would leave the park if he saw me there. But he accosted me at the Tubs. Instead of rejoicing at my good-luck, I asked after his wife. He left me standing there helplessly with an erection.

An Israeli soldier fellated me. He was a good kisser but he gave me mumps he had picked up from his little nephew. A kindly Arab doctor treated me for orchitis (my testes had grown to the size of a small grapefruit) but it left me sterile.

An Ethiopian priest would come to the gay park dressed only in a black cassock. We could not see him in the dark: black on black. He would spring a surprise upon us in the bushes; throw up his cassock over his head, bend over and offer his glorious black bum to any passers-by.

At the Ethiopian Church, a white St George lancing the dragon (of rumour) in the ear!

Just down from the orthodox Jewish Quarter is the Mikvah or the Ritual Bath. Jews use it on Saturdays, Arabs on Fridays; the gays congregated there Mondays and Tuesdays. Golda Meir had the old Arab hamam in the Walled City blown up to kill an Arab terror-leader. Arab and Jew and gay found solace in Mea Shearim's Mikvah. It had a sun roof, hot and cold baths, a steam room with old stone beds, a windowed vault which let in daylight, an Arab room with rugs and cushions. It was owned by an Arabic-speaking Jew from Baghdad who valued me as long as I had a job as a teacher. Mikvah students came there to fellate Arabs. Israeli soldiers came there to bugger the Arab boys who worked there as cleaners. Israelis tired of bearing the whip willingly became sex slaves to Arabs momentarily in bed. Orgies ensued in the basement boiler room at dusk on Tuesdays when the proprietor obligingly delayed the switching-on of lights. Sex and politics / sex and death. An intense searchlight was turned on by conducting our privatest of acts in public spaces. And in the dusk at the bathhouse with shades searching shades, it seemed as if bodies begged for souls.

At the Baths I met Mike, twenty, a New York Jewish Portnoy transplanted to Jerusalem. He lived with a fat Israeli girl but was gay. He fellated me and took me home to his water bed when his girlfriend wasn't home. He lived in the labyrinthine old Jewish quarter besides Jaffa Street, the line dividing east and west Jerusalem.

I met a South African Jewish lawyer. He was married. He carried a 'brolly' and always talked of making some 'lolly'. He was tall, thickset, bald, married and vegetarian. He ate young men with a relish. Wrote poetry. His wife accused him of trying to be 'interesting'. She, too, was fat and did not mind him being gay.

Ran Shinar was another South African by way of Delhi.

Jerusalem

His engineer father, of Moroccan Jewish descent, had built the Bhakra-Nangal Dam and had died of exhaustion in India. Ran learnt Kathak and befriended Hindu boys. 'Yeh to hamari galli ke Krishna aur Balram hai,' the Hindu housewives would say of the gay boys in their neighbourhood. Ran restored old arks at the synagogue. You lay gold leaf on wood and polish it in with a horn. Hard work. He lived behind Jaffa street in an old Arab house hung with textiles from India. He was into young boys. He had another South African friend whose Indian 'ayah' had converted him to Hinduism. He called himself a 'Hinjew'! Trying to illegally cross overland into India from Pakistan he was jailed there for three years. He and an Anglo-Indian boy from Goa made love for three years in jail, which made it bearable. I sought paying-guest lodgings with his mother.

She was an embittered, fat, lonely woman. Her drunk ex-husband would come home and sing in the shower:

I don't want her
You can have her
She's too fat for me!

When provoked she called all Indians 'coolies'. 'The British drowned Jewish refugee boats,' she'd say.

I was unemployed. I brought immigrant Jews from all over the world to my bed by day while my landlady worked. I remember a beautiful Sephardic Jew from Brazil. I gave him lice picked up at the sauna. Both of us had to cut our beautiful hair and delouse ourselves.

A British 'hajja' at school was after my job. She lived in a 'zwaita' with a Sheikh. The Sheik had finger-fucked Ran's dancing partner during her stint as a Moslem convert from American Jewry. So I too had something on them! Consider it a 'tahara' (purification), the 'hajja' had advised the offended woman. Her son, a convert to Islam, took my job and taught 'God' in the English Department. They had links with the old Mufti of Jerusalem, who was our Chancellor. When I shook hands with the old, frail man I did not know I had shaken a firebrand's hands who'd shaken hands with Hitler. Politics! My enemy's (Jews') enemy (the Nazi) is my friend, the Arabs said.

I was an agnostic then. The Moslem science students talked of a static, creationist universe. I taught them 'entropy'. Science had answers. Some Arab scientists accepted them. As for faith, that was 'supra-rational'.

Shaul Shaked was the Zoroastrian scholar at Hebrew University. He said all the three great Western religions learnt Abraham's monotheism (actually, Akhenaten's). Once I met him at the movies with his friend, the 'civilian' Governor of the West Bank who had returned to academics. Shaked told the Arabist how the loyalty oath introduced by him, the Arabist, during his governorship had caused my job-loss. And both laughed heartily at me.

Israeli society, in spite of its colonisation of the West

Bank, was deeply democratic. Everyone stood in line at lunch time for their food. Once, I jumped the queue at Hebrew University as I was late for class. They dragged me back to the end of the line! Israelis dance on the rim of a volcano. Their 'colonies' afford them cheap labour and ample profit. On the Netanya beachfront I saw middle-class, middle-aged women wave bravely to Israeli boys going off to bomb Beirut in 1982. At a chic sun-roof restaurant I was once served a huge strawberry and cream. 'Last days of the Roman Empire!' I exclaimed. 'First days of the Jewish Empire!' retorted the campy waiter. The great Israeli poet, Yehuda Amithai disappointed me when he spoke: 'I reach for a gun before I answer my door!' I had loved his love poems.

The poetry of the Holy Land: Nablus is the Biblical Sechem. On Mt Gerizim Moses stood and glimpsed the Holy Land but died before he could enter it. At Beit Lehem Jacob slept in the Potter's Field, a stone for a pillow and dreamed of a ladder to Heaven. At the Holy Mount I saw the stone on which Abraham started to sacrifice his hapless son, Isaac; the wooden frieze donated by the Knights Templar; below is the Wailing Wall, the only remnant of King Solomon's Second Temple. At the Church of the Holy Sepulchre I saw a small rocky mound, Golgotha. The Seven Stations of the Cross wend through the way donkeys wend through even today:

> O fools! For once I too had my hour
> One far, fierce hour and sweet

When there were shouts about my ears
And palms below my feet.
—G.K. Chesterton, 'The Donkey'

The Gate through which Jesus entered in triumph; the window where Herod pronounced 'Ecce Homo'; the Crusaders' gate with Richard Lionheart's emblem of the Three Flying Lions on a pennant... The Church of St Mary was actually a Venus Temple decorated with seashells; the Samaritans still practised blood sacrifices and magic and women drew water from the well where Jesus promised Eternal Waters.

Then there are the daily miracles: of the Lubban Valley on the way to Jerusalem from Nablus with almonds in flower, the fallen petals dyeing the grass beneath each almond tree a deep pink, almost purple. The Land of Milk and Honey. Thrown up from the bed of the prehistoric sea, Tethys.

I had to lie that I was Moslem to be able to enter the Dome of the Rock before Friday prayers. 'Nablus' was really 'Neopolis' of the Romans. It was a centre for the olive, almond, and fig trade. Decadent, no doubt. Up until the 40s it had an elite homosexual Arab culture flourishing with the likes of Ibrahim Touqan and his circle of intimates. But now the Revolution forbids intimacy.

I broke all taboos: I loved men and women. Mahar Khayyat, a student leader rusticated from Abu Dis, touched me deeply. His mother was disappointed in him: she had sold her 'oud' (lute) to send him to school. His twin sister 'Mahera' had been jailed for blowing up a bus on the road to Israel. She found freedom in a prisoner swap. She joined Laila Khaled in Paris. Maher dreamt of going to meet her but the Israeli authorities denied him the right of return; one of thousands of such cases. I would visit him each afternoon after school. I lent him dinars, to support his small hosiery shop, which he duly returned. His elder brother even bought a secondhand car with it. I can see Maher's slim waist, long arms and legs, small toes, big hands, pear-shaped buttocks, long nose, blue eyes, bushy eyebrows, white skin, large ears, thin lips hiding an overbite, cleft chin, the seven-o-clock shadow on his fair cheek. So closely had I observed him hour upon hour; and he, me. Writing this description I feel like the humble Bengal potters who fashion a god out of mere clay and hence come to be on easy terms of familiarity with a godhead. Maher knew I loved him passionately. His compassion prompted him to stay in the shop overnight on my last night in Palestine. I felt shy and I broke the tryst. I did not want the only Platonic love of my life to kiss the dust.

Suha was the sister of Maher's friend. She was also at Abu Dis. Once I chanced upon her and we chatted about Anais Nin. Later I gifted her *Under A Glass Bell*, which I bought on Jaffa street. She fell in love with me. She was small, dark, and compassionate but also committed politically, something I hadn't guessed. Her brother asked Maher what I wanted from her. Maher being shy couldn't say, 'they're romantically involved,' so he said, 'Hoshang wishes to marry Suha.' The brother would've harboured his sister's secret. But I made a tactical mistake. I visited her house one afternoon and proposed marriage. Her father came home from office and practically drove me out of the house. But Suha and I remained friends. Her objection wasn't that I wasn't Moslem nor Arab but that I hadn't joined the PLO! It is a life-and-death situation that every man, woman and child faces in Palestine and there's no time for frivolity. 'Friendship is the only sweetness in our lives,' Suha would say. She was angry when her brother brought home a second wife over the first wife's head. But she was amused when the often women became friends and made common cause against their husband's chauvinism. Survival strategies!

BURAK
We went under the arches
He and I
We bowed our heads
He and I
under a great moon
glowing over the old city
He took my hand
His in mine
We bent our heads
He and I
The dome glowed silver

all for us
The dome glowed gold
all for us
The city slept
Unlike us
We roamed and roamed
He and I
Our fate was doomed
His and mine
We exchanged breaths
He and I
We exhaled words
He and I
Our beings took flight
His and mine

On a steed
Neither male nor female
To a place
Neither earth nor paradise
We bowed our heads
Under the arches
because our fate was doomed
His and mine

Actually I was romantically involved then with Fayez, a student of mine. He was older than his class and sexually experienced. He slept with me out of friendship. I helped him pay his fees. The PLO had sent him to Athens but they demanded he eventually join their politics which he wouldn't do. So he was left helpless. He loved a rich heiress at school. He naively hoped to marry her. The desire of the moth for the star. She was the modern Arab girl: Fashionable, virginal and politically active. As I had predicted she married someone else. Fayez was heartbroken. But I could only laugh out loud in his face. When they knew about my involvement with Fayez at school from their spies, they kicked both of us out. With my bonus salary I sent Fayez to Hebrew University. There he slept with all his young Jewish female teachers and got cent per cent marks in all subjects. (He knew Hebrew, having lived in Jerusalem among Jews.) He'd probably worked in Athens as a male prostitute to make ends meet. 'You know,' he told me, 'When we were young we could do anything just for a pack of Marlboros!' He would come to me smelling of woman, covered with a woman's nail-marks and bites. He'd apologise. Then make love to me. I worked as a toilet cleaner and garbage picker at a Jewish Youth Hostel. But Fayez was good in bed, I loved him, and that made everything seem just fine for a while. At least I wasn't whoring at the baths or at the gay park.

I would earn a dollar a day. I'd beg meals from guests (mostly women) and repay them with a poem. At week's end I'd buy a book for $3.50 and see a movie for $3.50 at the Edison Cinema next door. I saw *Carmen* thrice in three weeks. I loved opera and wept each time at the flower-song, remembering Fayez's infidelity.

Once I became deathly ill for a day after cleaning up the vomit of a tourist who'd visited an Egyptian pyramid sealed for a thousand years. I was fine after the bug left my body in a day. The neighbour was a professor's widow; her son too taught at Hebrew University. She rightly hated all the commotion the young made at the hostel and directed her hostility at me: 'A professor who picks garbage!' She'd snort in my face and slam her door on me. I'd recite 'Lucy Grey' as I took the stinking garbage to the municipal trash bin telling myself unsuccessfully about mind over matter! Once a duo of young Jewish musicians played a violin and viola sonata (perhaps by Brahms) for me in the stairwell at midnight. I sat atop the winding stairs where the crescendo rose. So, too, did neighbour. End of concert.

Gloria, a divorcee from Panama, travelled the world on $700 a month her American ex-husband gave her. She was pushing forty but was petite with lithe figure, firm breasts, and a peroxide blonde Afro hairstyle. Bus drivers solicited her routinely. Once we shared LSD and a shower together. Gloria had Hispanic morals. She'd go with you but she wouldn't go all the way. She pitied me. I'd remove her toenail polish with acetone. I too was devoted to her. She was wild. She'd thrown a carving knife at her husband when she'd discovered him with another woman. Fayez wanted to sleep with her. 'But he's bald!' she protested. Fayez's vanity was hurt.

Yasmin was a 'pocket Venus'. Men followed her in the streets. 'It's your eyes,' her grandma from Sidon would say. She and a friend would sit in the class and cruise the young male teachers' boxes, she told me. She had an Arab photographer who'd put her on a table in his studio and give her oral sex. Her nose was crooked, to one side; her brother had broken it with a hockey stick. 'You have Madhubala's body and Nadira's face,' I'd mock her. She had told her grandma about me so grandma dreamed of us at a picnic beside a fountain; happy together!

This was not the first time Fayez had tried to nick in on my women. I was so devoted to him I'd let him do anything to me. But the women knew him better. My student Yasmin pursued me and finally succeeded in getting me in bed with her. Suha hated her. We dated for six months. We'd end up at my Naomi street bedsit (where Fayez visited also) after class and make love every single afternoon. My Jewish neighbour, a concert pianist, would practise modern music like Ravel's or Faure's on the piano. The wild music would be carried on the afternoon land breezes and would be a fitting background to our wild lovemaking. Yasmin was a clitoral woman and demanded full attention. Our neighbour's balcony abutted my window. So busy would I be in bed I wouldn't notice my curtain billowing on the breeze affording my young neighbour a full ringside view. He'd be grateful for our performance, too, and wouldn't shy away even when we caught him at his voyeuristic pleasures. He was a Sabra probably and his free morality belonged to the Kibbutz and the Israeli Army which recruits women, hippies, gays.

I would marry Yasmin. I became a Moslem.

The young Ramallah mullah would exchange English lessons for lessons on Islam.

'To marry woman is not reason to be Moslem!'

'Do you believe in God?'

—'I've heard he exists.'

'In Mohammed?

—'He was a historical reality.'

Say after me:

La Ilahi: Illallah

Mohammed al Rasool-ullah

I repeated the 'kalima'. I was Moslem.

'You can't believe Buddha now.'

—'OK!'

'Also your Zoroastrian gods of your fathers'.

I said 'yes' with a pang for lost gods.

Two witnesses fed me kunafeh in the marketplace. Ramadan: fasting and praying. I could never fast and pray. Though I still pay 'zakat' to the mosques and I never take interest on my money.

How do I un-become a Moslem?

—'You don't, said Maher.

—'A Parsi, Buddhist, Christian gay Moslem!' sister mocked me.

My sister had prepared a basement room for us in her Chicago home. I had an American visa but our honeymoon-money went for Fayez's Israeli degree and Yasmin and I parted bitterly when Fayez tried to ingratiate himself to her by telling her I was gay and that she should prefer him to me. She retorted, 'I love Hoshang for what he is'. Fayez came back, rather stunned, to tell me, 'She really loves you!' Her family was no help. Her mother hated me. 'He looks like a postman with his bag!' Her father thought she'd be forced back into the kitchen if she married me and went with me to what he thought was 'a backward country' like India. Her sister was then studying medicine in Russia and had a Russian boyfriend unknown to the parents. She'd try to fob off her Arab suitor on Yasmin. 'An Arab doctor comes every evening in his Mercedes Benz to take me out. He wants to marry me. What shall I do?' Yasmin wrote in a letter to me.

—'Marry the doctor. I'll never own a Benz', I wrote back.

I broke Yasmin's heart. She probably married and broke all contact with me.

That was my last chance to marry at thirty-six.

—'It was not fated to be', said an Indian astrologer to me.

The hostel owner also owned a bar on Jaffa street (Yaffo in Hebrew). English girls who doubled as waitresses lived free at the hostel. A barman, an Israeli with a British passport routinely stole money from the bar safe, money kept for safekeeping by unsuspecting lodgers, and from the luggage left at the hostel when the visitors went sightseeing by day. He was probably gay. We discovered a noose in the loft where he slept. He 'dated' the English waitresses to ward off any suspicion he was otherwise. I lost two passports and $500 at the hostel. When sister sent $500 and I kept it in the bar safe, that too went missing. So I doubled as glass washer in the bar by night. I lasted a day. I was to stay strictly in the kitchen. But by midnight my curiosity piqued me so I came out into the bar. I saw two burly men wrestling each other to the ground. 'Make love not war!' I said, much to the hilarity of the other drinkers.

All religions say, 'Thou shalt not steal', including Buddhism. All religions are money based, for the moneyed bourgeois. Since I was stolen from, I stole petty cash from the hostel till for my boyfriend. 'If you're stolen from, you will steal.' I had broken the last bourgeois taboo; against theft. I could also now say I had done everything for love including stealing money. The management sent Gloria to quiz me but I did not confess. She gave up on me and packed me a picnic basket for my sea journey to India via Greece. I was down to my last shekels.

I had to go overland to Jaffa instead of taking the ferry to Athens across the Mediterranean where my Air India Jet to Bombay awaited me. Jaffa had banyan and plumeria brought from India and transplanted in Mandate Palestine by the British. The heat and crow shit. I could have been walking in Bombay already. White plumeria was mother's favourite flower. I also chanced upon Queen's Lace which the Arabs call 'Al-Quodsi' after Jerusalem. Its pungent smell was the pervading smell in our childhood playground in Bombay at the mill-workers' tenement where father lived with mother. Now he lived with his new wife on an upmarket Bombay beach in a posh apartment. I really had no home to go to. I wept and wept on the boat all the way to Athens.

When the boat pulled out of Haifa harbour at sunset we saw the Dome and cypresses of Bahaullah's Mausoleum on the receding shoreline. Baha'is were a creation of the British, to break the Shiite mullahs' might in Iran in the early twentieth century. So it was fitting the British found him a grave in British Mandate Palestine. A traitor and an exile.

The light at Patmos next evening was ethereal. It broke from the clouds. St John wrote the Gospel here. The very air was holy. I cheered up. All was not lost. Not yet.

The Adonises at the Athens Museum reminded me of Fayez's lithe, sculpted body. I sent him an Adonis postcard telling him that. 'Thank you,' he wrote back. That was the last I heard from him. I learnt from friends he was in America. So was Ran Shinar, who had predicted nothing but doom for me and had broken friendship with me in my hour of need lest I mooch off him.

Some British tourists invited me to Olympus. I had to pass up the chance as my last $200 I had to keep as fees for a Bombay lawyer to claim my inheritance from mother who had been dead twenty years already.

'Do not bring any of your prostitutes here,' stepmother told me when I asked her if I could marry Yasmin and bring her home. I changed the subject and never broached the topic again.

What I remember of Palestine I press into these pages. The Fat Poet wanted to take me back to Nabil; to go with me to teach in Brunei now that I had publicly refused loyalty to the PLO by putting my name on an Israeli loyalty oath. Of course, I refused. The Jerusalem office of *Al-Fajr* (the Dawn), the only English language Arab paper in the West Bank where I first read a translation of Genet's 'A Visit to Sabra and Shatila', still welcomed me. But the new-generation politician, Barghouti (now in an Israeli jail) refused to shake hands with me. The generation of Zohair and Rashda was kinder. Zohair died recently. After my letters to Rashda went unanswered for years I finally got a letter from her personal assistant

'Rashda Masri died in 1990.'

With her died Mandate Palestine and the generation of accommodators, finally. She suffered from cancer and had had a mastectomy. Among my sister's papers I found a request for a prosthetic bra from Rashda. 'I want it for a cousin,' she'd characteristically written. When she invited me home one last time Rashda fed me stuffed kusa (marrow) and pilaf under a portrait of her dad emblazoned: 'Our Father who Art in Heaven!' We had never come out of the playpen and now I was returning to mine . . .

I would like to end my Palestine Diary with a memory of my first day in Palestine. The children on my street 'adopted' me readily. They asked me to join their picnic to the Sea of Galilee for which they had hired a taxi. I was to be their guest. I, of course, spoke no Arabic and we communicated in pidgin. I sat on the beach all day in my street clothes as I had forgotten to pack my swimming trunks. The boys swam, played and fished. Their fishing was indeed cunning. They drugged the fish with opium (mukkhaddar) which they sprinkled on the waters; then simply picked up the dead fish with their bare hands. Among all the chaos I felt inexplicably lonely, lacking not only language but any connection to a new place. In my silence I heard the waves lapping on the shore; I heard my own heartbeats and the gasps of the fish flapping their fins on the sand. I felt oneness with the universe. As we left at night a full moon rose over the lake, illuminating the water, and a gentle breeze set up spumes of watery spray. On the breeze I thought I saw Jesus walking upon the waves.

> The body is bound
> Jesus travels, a spirit, on the waves
> —Rumi (Arberry translation)

Another memory is of Fayez and me at a school picnic at Pan's Grotto in the occupied Golan Heights of Syria. The young Litani river is forced out at great speed with a roar echoing through a rocky glen. Hence, Pan's grotto. Fayez had the habit of picking the biggest blossom in a garden for his lady love. All day I sulked alone seeing him walk with his heiress; a big, purple rose in hand. The deafening roar of the river increased my panic. At picnic's end Fayez gave me the rose. I cast it on the waters.

FAIRUZ SINGS 'LEBANON'

Again after five years
And I listen with the pores
of my skin
I listen with the wounds
I gave Lebanon
And Lebanon gave me
I listen with the voice of Fairuz
I listen with her ears
and with her eyes
the voice of exile divorce sorrow
and more sorrow
I love you
My love my love my love my love
Why have you left me alone?
Your valleys I love
goodbye to the almond trees
of Lebanon
I listen with the voice
of the boys

who fall out of olive trees
who mingle with its streams
who become each stone and pebble
of Lebanon
Who die die
who translate for me
Their Lebanon
Their love love love
How can I leave it alone?
To remember it is to open a wound
To leave it is to open a wound
Fairuz: I'm that bleeding wound
Israel lays siege again to the Beaufort of my heart
I surrender: not everyone is meant for martyrdom

My final image of Palestine is Jean-Jouve's:
   Do not speak to me
   of golden domes
   The angel-lovers of Jerusalem . . .
   Tell me of two steps we took
   Joining our hands
   in the faltering darkness.

                                        Hyderabad
                                          2008

Garden of Bliss

Prologue

21 February 1999 (Anaïs Nin's birthday)

It is all a matter of concentration: If you concentrate on knowledge you become a wise man; if on money, a rich man; if on love, a prostitute but if you concentrate on god you become a saint.
—S. Radhakrishnan, Commentary on Gita

Every great document of civilization is at the same time a document of great barbarism. And when this document changes hands each transfer is marked by great violence.
—Walter Benjamin, 'Essay on the Philosophy of History,' in *Illuminations*

Sex is a way to sainthood.

—Anaïs Nin, *Diary III*

Why I write

I

'As everyone knows by now, I'm homosexual.' To write this sentence and to speak it publicly, which is a great liberation, is why I write. How did I write my first poem? I was beaten up while cruising the streets of a small university town in Michigan, one summer in the early 1970s. The man was a Chicano, a migrant Mexican labourer, nameless, of course. He wanted everything: love, money, food, sex, just as I did then because I was a poor student in the world's richest democracy. I remember the room we made love in. I went into the kitchen to make tea, a light liqueurish Darjeeling which smelt of home. He stole the Nepali knife I had hung on the wall to beautify my rented room and tried it on the writing desk, cracking it from side to side. Was this the man I had made love to five seconds before? Was he a brute or a human being? Did I not wish to go over from my effete life into the vitalism of his life? Had I not stolen his manhood by stealth in a bed? Was he not justified in wishing me dead?

'12 red roses splattered the shiftfront of my chest.'
—Lorca

The next night I could not sleep. I had stitches on my nose, slowly healing. But I was afraid of the dark. I changed my night lodgings. I slept in a different room the next night. I did not want my private terror to pursue me. In the morning I awoke to Josephine Jacobsen reading on the radio:

All need is dry / Rain is a metaphor.
Sex is a metaphor. A poem is a metaphor.
Love is a poem; a made thing.
And a poem is love; a communication.
I am not mad. I write in order not to go mad.

Zen is the art of not committing suicide, not going insane, not becoming a cripple.
—Suzuki, *Zen Buddhism*

(I learnt much later that Josephine Jacobsen, consultant in poetry to the Library of Congress, was crippled at birth).

There are no birds this year
In last year's nest

I'm sane now
Then, I was mad.

—Basho, 'Haiku'

II

I'm in a different room now. My mother has suddenly become a cripple. She cannot walk since the day father left her for another woman. I am sixteen. I know there is a lesson somewhere in this.

And I go back into this mansion of memory with rooms within rooms. And I'm a child of five. I'm sick with malaria. It is 1952 and all the quinine won't work for this soul sickness.

I am in love with my mother.

She has a soft green kimono of mercerized cotton which always smells clean, and her long hair is soft. This mansion of memory could be my rich father's house on the sea at Bombay or it could be my mother's womb, the only place where I remember being truly happy.

My mother gives me her breast. A rich creamy soft breast. She lets me suckle long because I'm her only son.

Many years later I had a vision of the Phaeneromeni Mother, in Nicosia, Cyprus while awaiting a visa to Israel. She gave the Christ child a rich creamy soft breast. Phaeneromeni means the One Who Appears. The Divine

Mother appeared to me and led me to the Promised Land just as my mother had led me up the staircase of sorrow leading to Bandra's Mount Mary in Bombay.

III

Now I'm in a different room of memory. I'm twenty-three. I'm in Virgil Lokke's office at Purdue University saying 'I do not want to die before knowing everything.' Virgil led Dante through Hell. Surely there must be a way out of this mess I made of my life at twelve! And now Virgil is dead.

He was to me a father I never had. I had a father who laughed at a son who wrote poems instead of making money. He also frowned at daughters who did not marry, but praised their money making. My sisters and I were born modern, in independent India. But my poor father, who lost his doctor father at birth to the 1917 world epidemic of influenza, was brought up by an adoptive grandfather who was a wealthy but illiterate jeweller living in fear of an Avestan god and of Victorian morality.

Before her marriage my mother taught Gujarati in a Parsi school, sang Indian ragas, wore homespun for Gandhi and discussed Adyar's theosophy. Father put paid to all that. I identified with my mother's suffering.

So the first poem I wrote was on a photograph of the woman painter Georgia O'Keefe:

Gnarled, snarled hands
And light on the temple
A world is not given
But made.

It was not about life but about art. I was about life-in-art. Then came along Anaïs Nin saying pretty much the same thing. It was the Mother, the woman-artist who caught me and liberated me.

IV

When Venice was a village Isfahan was a world-empire.
Isfahan, nesf-e-jehan
Isfahan is half the world. Now I'm in the Sophy's palace. I wander through the music room. Why was a king called the Sophy? Because he was a Sufi. He owned nothing. He held everything in trust for God.

When I gave up my father's wealth, because homosexual sons don't inherit, I gained the world.

Jalal-ud-din Rumi and Shams-i-Tabrizi. The teacher and student as lovers. Shams was murdered on his way to Mecca, and Rumi poured out his heart in poems. 'Separation leads to pain,' is the first teaching of Zen Buddhism, of Sufism, of Christianity which speaks of a Fall. Rumi was God-drunk and he danced and sang of the Return to Wholeness describing vast circles in space with his body.

I travelled to America, Iran, India, Tibet, Arabia, Palestine, Israel, Italy, Britain, Germany—vaster and vaster circles in space. I travelled like Rama for fourteen years.

I lost my innocence in Iran. My hair turned white almost overnight. Saw killing in the streets with my own eyes. A boy lifted his hand to throw a stone. He was met with the soldiers' machine-gun fire. His hand was blown off. He was brought badly bleeding from the groin to the carpet shop where I had hid. The stench of the fresh young blood oozing purposelessly on those priceless carpets! In Iran, in Kurdistan, in Palestine, this same blood springs up as poppies in the fields at spring.

I learnt to love my students as Shams loved Rumi.

V

On 19 February 1999 my teacher was murdered in Bombay. Mehroo Jussawalla lived alone, a spinster from one of the city's leading legal families. She taught us moral values culled from Spenser. She was murdered by a brute in her sleep. I wrote her a poem:

The Loneliness of My Spinster Teacher

The staircase would humorously creak
To bear your load
And you would laugh out loud
At the wooden protest

Garden of Bliss

O that this too too solid flesh would melt!
That was no cosmic joke!
And the table groaning
Under mountains of food
And the full belly laughing at noon

There were other things under other suns
The Oxford girl reading Marvell or Donne
These hands were not meant for work or the kill
But only to prise a meaning out of a text
Her father's own Penelope

And the cobwebs and the tapestry
The warp and woof of familial love
(Mother dead)
The weevil in the bin at work
The termite in the leather bookbinding

Ruskin, Venice and the honeyed sun of love
Sinking over Malabar Hill
The evenings longer
The laughter sharper
And then the night

(On the map
Bombay is a hand
But it is actually an open mouth)

Coda:

There was this healthy woman
With a disease, so lonely
That grew and grew

And the working-class thief
Who came up at night to kill
Was really a redeemer . . .

The branch is bent when green
And if not, then—

So I write to make sense of death.

What was Mehroo Jussawalla's crime? She hurt no one. She was dutiful daughter, a conscientious teacher. She did social service as the women of her class are wont to do. Miss Jussawalla's crime was that she could not see beyond her hilltop balcony to the slums below. In all probability a mafia landlord hired a slum dweller to axe her for her property. Walter Benjamin says that it is a fascist society that does not change property relations between social classes. Nazim Hikmet, whom I quote, writes:

The branch is bent when green
And if not, then—

So I am a teacher.

When Ramakrishna preached throughout India someone shouted from the crowd:

> Do something for the suffering people of India
> I CAN DO NOTHING, the master said.

'This is the position of the artist,' says Anaïs Nin, commenting on this episode.
'I have taken the warning to my heart. I couldn't, but my students will make the revolution.
When the revolution comes I will be the first one to be killed.' (Nin)

How I Write

I shut my bedroom door, unplug the phone and the radio, sit cross-legged like a yogi in the centre of my bed and write. I say:

Knowledge is what comes by osmosis in a bed
Or
My poems are written in bed
They are meant for *other's* heads

But this is just the final process. I write my poems on the streets, in buses, while shopping or teaching, in my head. As a medical student Zubin Mehta said a Brahms concerto was always running through his head as he cut up a dogfish.

Proust had his cork-lined room; Anaïs Nin her fireproof bunker. It is a luxury to say poets write about nature. They do not. They write about culture. It was a luxury for Kim Novak, the 50s movie-star to bathe in a sea-facing bathroom at her Big Sur home with polar bears for company. But I bet her neighbour, Henry Miller, would bolt at the sight of a bear. In fact he writes Nin from Corfu that he longs to be at the Opera. The modernist poet is a citified being. As I wrote:

> In a city where behemoths
> Compete for space with buses
> The absence of poetry is also a poetry.

Poetry is not about Nature. It is about Homer. The poet ransacks the traditions. If I'm in Iran I read Sufi poetry rather than the Avesta because I need to make sense of the Other, as a Parsi I need to know the Moslem.

Enemy, my enemy I name you friend. (Neruda)

Hart Crane tore around his New York City bachelor apartment crying: 'I am Baudelaire; I am Rimbaud; I'm Christ.' So the French poetry of symbolism comes naturally to anyone seeking to revolutionize sensibility. It did to Lorca, Crane, Nin, Ginsberg.

My first published poem, 'Circles', was based on the Soviet silent film 'Earth' by Dovzhenko:

> He died dancing
> Among harvest fruit
> His widow tore her weeds in grief
> And it rained
> Till the melons rotted

And the landlord who shot him
for a piece of land
Was so joy ridden
He stuck his head
In the mud
And danced in circles
Till he died.

I was trained in the West. I was not brought up on the *Shah Nameh*, which is the Persian epic, nor on the Hindu *Mahabharata*. I read Homer and about the Greek wars at school. I saw my warring Parsi family as cursed as the House of Atreus. At college I found an echo of my conditions in *A Streetcar Named Desire* or *A Long Day's Journey into Night*, in *Phaedra* first and only later in the epic of the hapless Siavosh accused wrongfully by his stepmother.

It is when we make our lives into myths that we find our true meaning. This is, of course, a paraphrase of Nin who might be paraphrasing Jung.

So our writing is marked by hybridity and mirror imaging: Echoes within echoes, box-within-box as in a Chinese box, mirrors mirroring mirrors in a fun house. To parody Leonard Cohen:

Giving head in a hired bed
With the taxi throbbing in the street

How else do I make sense of the boys I bed? No, I do not write to beautify them; I write in order to go over to them, as Pasolini did. So there is this great democracy of sex and death, Whitman knew, and Lorca, and poor Wilde, and of course, Pasolini. And the boys we dream of come out of the Old City slums or from the recently bourgeoisified proletariat. They all imitate Shah Rukh or Salman, Saif or Aamir, the four reigning Khans of Bollywood. And, as I teach Kubla Khan, I dream him and become him in my poems.

Just as my mother was the 1940s tragediennes Meena Kumari or Nargis with her tears, I was the 1960s gamins Sadhana or Saira at sixteen being wooed in Bombay's overcrowded suburban trains. If this sounds weird, I'm conscious of it. Art does not imitate life as Arnold was silly enough to believe, but it is life that imitates Art as Wilde saw it in *The Decay of Lying*.

What is the relation of a homosexual artist to his body? Poems are written on the body. Ask the English painter Francis Bacon or the Japanese gay Zen poet, Takahashi. My student writes about my work in *Deccan Chronicle* in 1994: 'Hoshang Merchant has a beautiful body.' (You can now change that 'has' to 'had.') Nin was beautiful into her sixties. Ginsberg was photographed nude by Richard Avedon with his handsome lover placed behind him so that we see the hippie poet's large belly and largish member delicately cut out of the frame. Or, take the gay Mapplethorpe's photographs of the body. Once in a Greenwich Village gallery I saw a gay artist mount a cross in the nude to complete his real-life sculpture entitled 'The Crucifixion'. In a Japanese film on the relation between silence and the spoken mantra in Zen Buddhism, the entire sutra was tattooed on the live body of a monk to the beating of gongs, lighting of fires, loud chanting, and of course the monk's screams. But these are extreme examples. Yet no one is surprised to read at school that Poe was found dead naked on the city's busiest thoroughfare one morning, a bodily sacrifice to the bitch-goddess who devoured him for hymning the moon goddesses.

The gay Parsi poet's body and language are colonized by Parsi culture first and then by the dominant culture he inhabits in India or Iran or the West—by heterosexual notions of sexuality, by colonial history. Zoroastrianism, Hinduism, Islam, Christianity all forbid homosexuality. The men we sleep with in childhood are married men who are heterosexual or bisexual.

The language we speak at home is a hybrid Parsi/Gujarati born out of the long love of the Parsi for his Gujarati neighbour. We took to English like ducks to water but we lost our language a second time and we stand accused of 'chamchagiri' (toadyism) towards the British. The case of Kafka comes to mind. An Austrian Jew, he spoke Yiddish but wrote in German to his eternal shame and glory.

One way for me to rejoin India was translation. I came

to Urdu through Hindi, Persian, Arabic: the languages I picked up on my travels.

Art is to be lived, not merely read. Now that is a dangerous proposition leading to the madhouse and to death.

Well, how *does* one write?

I write very quickly. And if it gels so much the better. If it doesn't *tant pis*. 'First said, best said,' Ginsberg believed. I rewrite a trauma over many, many years until it crystallizes. This is how I could finally write about my parents' divorce or a sister's abortion. Nothing is laboured, everything is spontaneous. 'Poems come like leaves to trees.'

I'm fifty, and the nation is fifty and we have to make sense of each other. What is a gay poet saying to a half-starved nation where rape occurs every ten minutes and a child is born every minute? Perhaps that sex cuts across caste and class? How do you write gayness when there is no gay culture? How you create a gay aesthetic for urban India?

I found my answer in Pound, a poet's poet. Pound said that if you can rely on high art to be really high then the tenor of popular culture wouldn't be so low. We wouldn't be subject to a garish TV *Ramayana*, which nonetheless funnels Hindu pride. Instead we would have our modern gay lives depicted with all the abandon that characterizes any true epic.

I've always spoken in rhymes. Still do I rely on my blood's rhythm, which is the rhythm of our spoken Indian English, the sea-rhythms of my births, of the tides and the moon-phases . . . the rhythm I first heard in my mother's belly.

Epilogue

'Do not forget the wisdom of our mothers,' Mulk Raj Anand wrote a young Hoshang in Tehran. 'Is Hoshang a gay poet or a Sufi Poet?' people now ask.

Think of the gay Jesuit who wrote 'Windhover', think of the *Divan-i-Shams-i-Tabrizi*, think of mad Sarmad followed by his boy from Sind to Golconda to Delhi, think of Amir Khusro making the Mogul prince Dara Shikoh so mad that Aurangzeb had to kill Dara, think of St John of the Cross on that dark and lonely night when a stranger pursues him up the narrow steps of his house, think of Takahashi dying of hunger in opulent modern Japan, think of the last poems of Ginsberg gone over to Elizabethan love-lyrics and the sweet Lord Buddha.

So the Urdu ghazal has crept into my Indian English poems. At the end of his life, Ghalib writes:

Apart from Allah all is vague
And nonexistent. There is no
Poetry and no poet, no ode and
No ode writer. Nothing exists
except God.

It seems to me the only god in my books and books of poems is the poem, i.e., it is the poem itself.

Ghalib also writes: Whatever happens to the mystic is good for his soul.

A comment on this is that madness is but the last stage of longing, be it for justice (the rage for it turning into violence) or for love, as with the beloved and blessed Sufi, Majnun.

In Hindu Bhakti literature we have a term 'Radha-bhava.' It assumes, like all mysticism, that the divine principle is male, all others are female souls yearning for divine union. The Radha-bhava suits the spiritually inclined modern gay writer. It is not an accident that Winston Leyland of the Gay Press, San Francisco, is interested in the Iranian mysticism of Jalal-ud-din Rumi who is currently very fashionable in America in Coleman Bark's translation or mistranslation. This is not feminism: the story of Mirabai comes to mind. Tulsi Goswami refused to see her in Brindaban on the grounds that she was a woman. She sent word right back that she thought the only man in Brindaban was Lord Krishna and everyone else was only a woman. She was promptly granted an audience.

There is a well known thumri:

Tum Radha bano/Main banoo Shyam
(You be Radha/I Krishna)

Epilogue

When a man, Bhimsen Joshi, sings this, it is all very well. But when women like Parveen Sultana or Begum Akhtar sing it we get a special thrill. The same thrill when we recognize the beauty and terror of the Pichwai painting of Radhaji with Krishna's crown and Krishnaji in Radha's sari. It is the eunuch in my friend Bhupen Khakhar's painting: always naked, always an outcast, but with a sky-blue sari sewn with tinsel stars! Krishna is not 'bhogi' (sensualist), he is India's greatest yogi (ascetic). At first poetry is transgressive; ultimately it is transcendent:

> Bairam Khan was sent on a pilgrimage by Akbar
> Then set upon / So was Shams by Rumi's son
> No wonder they never returned
> But myths grow around madmen not kings
> They're said to become one with god
> Their blood waters the Martyr's Tree
> Its leaves turn books
> Boys become poets / Lovers become ascetics
>
> Yet people say: Love accomplishes nothing
> Sacrifice accomplishes nothing
> Politics is all / Ambition is all
>
> A benediction does not stop a gun
> But it shames the assassin for centuries
> What arms accomplish is immediate

Garden of Bliss

Ashes are for the whole world for aeons
The pelican feeds its young with its blood
Some call him Christ/Others, Mother
When Hindu killed Moslem I made love to a Moslem
Listen to me. Do not call me names
Now I've stopped speaking. There is nothing more to hear.

I Am not in

Th' expense of spirit in a waste of shame
Is lust in action; and till action, lust
Is perjur'd, murd'rous, bloody, full of blame.
Savage, extreme, rude, cruel, not to trust;
Enjoy'd no sooner but despised straight;
Past reason hunted, and, no sooner had,
Past reason hated, as a swallowed bait,
On purpose laid to make the taker mad—
Mad in pursuit, and in possession so;
Had, having, and in quest to have, extreme;
A bliss in proof, and prov'd, a very woe;
Before, a joy propos'd; behind, a dream.
All this the world knows; yet none knows well
To shun the heaven that leads men to this hell.
—William Shakespeare, Sonnet 129

I Am not in

Remember, you are a Karamazov—
from your father's side, you are all lechers;
and from your mother's, fools for Christ
 —Fr Zossima to Alyosha in Brothers Karamazov

Sex is a way to sainthood.

—Anaïs Nin

I

It is time to fill in the gaps in my autobiography: Especially what I did between the time I returned from Palestine and the time I got the teaching job in Hyderabad (1982–89): The seven-year Saturn transit.

    I returned to Pali Hill. It is painful. But I must tell it. Pali Hill was crumbling. My middle sister had attempted suicide a second time (unbeknownst to me). All the floors were dug up. The hexagonal red beehive tiles gone. During bouts of megalomania my sister thought to pave the bungalow with marble. 'A mausoleum!' I thought. A mausoleum to a family that was dead. Our family. I slept on the Rexine sofa, the old leather now replaced. The chandeliers long since gone, replaced by modern light-fixtures. The leaking roof of a huge bungalow repaired by sister on borrowed money. I paid her debt from the last money left from Israel: $1000 (then Rs 40,000). No money even to eat. Sister sparring with father over rights to the bungalow. I, caught in-between.

    I would spend time cooking simple dishes of my childhood: eggs spread on sautéed okra, potato or sweet and sour tomato. Father came one day: 'This is woman's work, Come to the factory!' I hated it. People warring over my loyalties, my soul.

Sister would be gone all day. She did not trust me with the house keys. Once I had to break into the house. Her lawyer phoned me and warned me I would be charged with 'trespass'. She had gone to court against father. I had refused to join her. Once she came home and started throwing casseroles of leftover food at me as I slept. Another night she stalked me to the bathroom, a heavy metal padlock in her hand concealed behind her, wishing to assault me so I would flee the house. All the tricks father had used against mother. Father assaulted her. I left the house on 'Bhai Dooj', day for brother–sister bonds.

I went to father's seashore apartment. Almost as soon as I entered stepmother's nagging started.

You want to live off your father's money!

I, who would not tolerate a wrong word against me from my own mother, listened to the stepmother's harangue for months.

She would cook for me, though.

'Treat her as a servant!' said my aunt who hated her brother's second wife more than she did the first. I was polite, even friendly, with stepmother.

It was time to get a job.

The great Indian job hunt:
Waiting in an anteroom with scores of poseurs.

One came with a suitcase full of his publications.

Another intoned there was an applicant from Heidelberg! (Me.)

A third tried to read the letter I was writing Yasmin:

'The long, snake-like train entered the dark tunnel . . . etc.' describing the journey from Bombay to Hyderabad through the Western Ghats as sexily as I could.

An arrogant professor dismissed me. A lady professor (a British woman married to a Bengali) on the recruiting committee kindly asked if I would come to her University in Calcutta. I said, 'No'. I had to be nearer to Bombay, to my dying father (the few years left to me to make amends). Of course, I did not get the job, nor did I get back my father!

Who should be in the berth opposite me on the return journey but the Peeping Tom! There was no avoiding him. He was Raj, going to Pune to inquire about a temporary vacancy at the University. Would I accompany him? Of course, I would! The Head of English, gave me the job, unasked, instead of to Raj! Our rivalry had started.

He accused me of eccentricity. He put it down to the fact of my being gay! (He was then in the closet.)

He took me to Bombay's Victoria Terminus to cruise the toilets. Mostly porters. I told stepmother. She told father.

'Drop him like a hot potato!' said father, of Raj.

I did.

The next time Raj called, father slammed down the receiver. (We later became literary friends.)

I stumbled on my sister Whabiz's unpublished papers on mother's first miscarriage with father. Father had kicked dead the child growing within mother because they were then not yet married. Father asked her not to publish it. Good writing. I wept to read it. I would henceforth forgive my sister any offence she gave me or to anyone else in the world. I have kept this promise to myself.

At Pune University I had to get back into the closet. This resulted in nightmares. A detective in a raincoat and fedora would follow me around the house in my dream. Each time the phone in my father's house rang, the detective would reach for it first and stop me from speaking the truth to my friends.

Mukti was an older student returning for a masters ten years into her marriage. (She had a French friend whom she subsequently married.) Mukti arranged for me to befriend one of her female classmates. (I was missing Yasmin with whom I corresponded. Sister would not forward any calls from Fayez when I lived with her at Pali Hill).

The day we arranged our tryst was Sports Day. The playing field was the only place where lovers got some quiet. But not that day! I could not take the girl to my official guesthouse room for fear of discovery. As we made our way out of a plumeria grove some men-students saw us. The girl fled home.

What did you two do, Sir?

I was in a mischievous mood. So I said:

'We sat under a tree. And I touched her all over!'

The die was cast. My prank was relayed all over the University. I had lost my job. Father was in no mood to take me back.

Mukti's parents found a room with a friend of theirs for me and fed me a square meal a day until I found a job. Mukti and I are still friends in Goa where she has retired.

Not that there was respect for me, ever, in Pune. The North Indian professors, among themselves, would refer to me as a 'Nautanki' (i.e. a cross-dresser). A colleague ratted to the Head that I had said the Head was jealous of my success with women. He was. The Head, now dead, played with young men's emotions. He would first love you to death and then hate you till you died. His elder son had indeed committed suicide. A brilliant younger son is rumoured to be gay.

Yet another colleague who wanted the vacancy I filled (for a PhD student of his) laid traps for me. He invited me home. The first time I did not show up sensing a trap. The second time I had to go. As he went out to bring home some beer he offered me a choice of reading material:

Playboy or *Playgirl*?! (*Playgirl* had nude male centrefolds.)

Playgirl! Playgirl! I clamoured. (A Bombay newsvendor had wailed: 'I can't get *Playboy*s, where will I get *Playgirl*s for you?!)

Once I lost my job, everyone wished to be my friend.

Just as at Hyderabad later, once everyone was promoted

over my head they all sought my friendship: some for professional reasons, some for social reasons; others, out of a feeling of spiritual affinity with me.

II

Mrs V was another kettle of fish. She was a once beautiful Pathare Prabhu Hindu lady who had lost her husband and son on the same day. She grieved and wept even to talk of it years after the event. They were aristocrats. Her husband had not worked a single day in his life, she said. An engineer by training he was friends with the Mysore Dewan Sir Visweswarayya. An invitation to tea from him graced her showcase of memorabilia. I roomed with her. She was a very gracious host to my Pune friends. She would remember exactly which way anyone liked his tea prepared if she had once served him tea. Under duress from a mean Parsi spinster-friend of hers she upped my rent. I had to take shelter with some other Parsi friends of hers. But Mrs V was a kind, even if unforgiving, lady. She taught me the Hindu Ganesha 'aarti': she would bathe the idol in water, with a quick swipe even at the god's behind just as a mother would while bathing an infant. Then she would light lamps, ring bells and offer sweets to him and to his two wives, Riddhi and Siddhi. I got to eat the sweets since Mrs V was dieting. I met her recently: she would not let me in but spoke to me through the iron door grill. She is eighty-five, she told me, and a great grandmother of a five-year-old girl. She would not accept my apologies for calling her names when she threw me out of her house but was genuinely glad I had made it to a professorship four years short of retirement. And she was genuinely saddened that father had written me out of his will.

Dinyar's family was afraid I would turn him gay. Dinyar was an heir to a Jalna cotton-fortune. Large hearted and weak minded, he was impressed by my learning. Shy by nature he enjoyed seeing the shock my outré behaviour created on his staid relatives whom he hated. The relatives had worked with the Nizam's government and the Parsi family (like the Hyderabad Vicajees) claimed to have bailed the Nizam out of debts. A tank in Jalna from Emperor Shah Jahan's time proclaimed on a tablet that it was built by Dinyar's ancestors. His cousins would be amused by me. The dumb one would sing the film song from *Anari* ('The Simpleton'):

Samajhne wale samajh gaye hain
Na samajeh woh Anari hai!
(i.e. only fools won't know etc.)

The brilliant one at the Armed Forces Medical College would say to me: 'Being homosexual is nothing but a brain's computer being wired wrong!' Mrs V wanted me to cook for

Dinyar. But I would not as I was already in love with Sharad, a Pune University science graduate. When Dinyar went in for appendicitis surgery his mother drove down from Jalna to Pune weeping all the way. She soon died of a heart attack. She was under pressure from her in-laws to separate Dinyar from me. I had to give up Dinyar's friendship. His family destroyed all my Pune writing (satires on Pune Parsis) when Mrs V was stupid enough to post the manuscript parcel I had left in trust with her to them.

Dinyar married a Parsi Gujarati village girl, has one son, has moved permanently to Pune where his widower father has built him a huge villa next to the Osho Ashram, Mrs V told me. She, however, withheld any further information lest I restart a friendship none approved of.

The last scene: I am to go to Hyderabad. I go to say my farewells to Mrs V. She is in the midst of arranging a welcome breakfast for Dinyar and his parents after his appendicitis operation. She asks me to stay. I stay. The mother turns on me:

When, in heaven's name will you leave Pune for Hyderabad?

'Am I a burden on you?' I counter.

The father joins the fray.

Do you not have any shame shouting at ladies?!

'A pox on both your houses!' I say and leave. The chauffeur, who had overheard the fracas, giggles as I leave.

When his son became of college age Dinyar phoned me.

I told him, Dinyar, I do not consider you my friend. 'WHY?' was all he said!

Each time his mother was rude to me he would defend her.

Which mother would like her only son to turn gay?

Actually the mother was much put upon by her in-laws in a joint family.

An Andhra boy offered me the floor of his Pune University hostel room to sleep on. 'Call me Kant,' he said. He was no philosopher but a good-hearted buffoon. He knew cruelty first hand being a Dalit Christian. He would bring hostel food to the room and feed me. I worked at a banking institute trying to bring humanities into management: I had to see Iago as an image of corporate intrigue, Lear as a kindly manager gone wrong. I was paid a pittance. The other Andhra boys confronted Kant. 'Throw Merchant out! He uses our toilets. We could catch AIDS!'

I had to go to the Pune Virology Institute and beg the director, a Parsi lady doctor to give me a free ELISA test. (I could not afford the Rs 100 fee.) She asked me why I needed it. I pretended I had just arrived from the Middle East. (The first Asian AIDS case was reported from Dubai). The male pathologist who took my blood sample figured out I was gay. He was rude enough to ask me if I was active or passive. To frighten him I said: 'I'm versatile'. That scared him off. But when I returned for my test-result the entire staff had turned upon the vestibule staircase leading to the upper floor—doctors on one side and nurses on the other—to gawk at a live, elite, self-confessed, passive gay, a rarity in Pune. They all snickered as I left with a negative report.

I wished to post my negative AIDS report on the hostel notice board. Kant asked I forgive the ignorant Andhra village boys. He soon asked me for sex. I refused. Kant had to forgive me then. Married later to a Moslem girl in a love marriage gone sour he asked me to mediate between them. I refused.

I was offered a one-year, temporary, pool officer's job at Hyderabad. I would not go as I had a bad experience with reappointment at Pune. I was also deeply in love with Sharad who would meet me most evenings. I could not return to father's.

The Last Scene at Father's: After losing my Pune job father had kept me on in the vain hope I would join his business. I was a thorn in his second wife's side who called me 'an enemy' to my face! When he left for eye surgery in America leaving me with her, she moved against me. (He had given her power-of-attorney over the factory.) He called me to ask me to go help at the factory. My instincts told me not to. As it turned out his assistant, behind his back, had stolen not only his business but also much equipment. So father had turned sour towards me. Stepmother, sensing a kill, accused me of theft, of Rs 40,000. Three days I heard her out with her threatening to call the police on the last day. I flung the Rs 2000 in 100-rupees notes father had left for me on her face and spat in her eye, for good measure.

'I never asked you why you entered our house, nor did I ever ask you how much you took. If I have taken Rs 40,000—which I have not—then it is my father's money I have taken and not yours,' I told her.

She phoned father and wept.

Your children are cruel to me.

Later she said she found the missing money in the car's glove compartment.

But her endgame succeeded. The day father returned from America he ordered me out of the house. I took a small bag of clothes, leaving my books and writing behind, and left immediately for Pune to my friends.'

Stepmother had learnt drama from Hindi films, an education for illiterate Indian women. Later, when I visited father's factory for the Diwali New Year he threw me out. I never stepped into his home again.

III (1989–2009)

After six months of holding on to Sharad and Pune I had to leave for Hyderabad. Makarand Paranjape was intensely jealous of me. Sudhakar Marathe did not want an openly gay instructor in 'his' department. Prof. Bh. Krishnamurti, vice chancellor, supported me throughout. Prof. S Viswanathan, then Head, told me not to worry so much about my sexuality.

—There but for the grace of God go I! he said. (A Victorian solecism I did not understand.) He also warned me of future exploitation.

Meenakshi Mukherjee and her elite feminist friends took umbrage because I did not subscribe to their brand of feminism or 'activism'. She remained an unrelenting enemy to the end. Even so, out of decency I attended her husband's funeral though I had not gone to my own father's.

I became Viswanathan's friend over poetry and Shaivism. (He cast my horoscope for me.) The painter Laxma Goud and I became friends over art. The ignorant could not understand what both men had in common with me. I still visit Viswanathan regularly in Madras. I still send him Siva poems. Laxma, in his eccentricity, has chosen to listen to his jealous associates and distanced himself from me though he did recently tell his Madras patron, a friend of mine:

'Hoshang is a great man. Hyderabad is too small to understand him.'

Knives were being sharpened for me and at the opportune moment they struck. A tale carrier found me in a student's bed at the Men's Hostel one night. My students occasionally invited me to stay overnight with them in a city wracked by riots or rains. They would vacate their room, go study and sleep in another room; I would leave the door unlocked so that they could access their things and I would sleep naked, as is my habit, in one of the students' beds.

'I found Hoshang sleeping naked in Saibaba's bed at midnight,' ran the written complaint. It forgot to mention Saibaba was not in the room and I slept alone. Everyone gloated at my imminent dismissal but I was let off with a warning. I had written a four-page 'confession' to my kindly boss on confirmation— I had to lie to get appointed—but I had neglected to mention that I would keep off my own students.

'Go seek friends in another university!' counselled the kindly boss.

Now everyone's got what he wanted, including me, and everyone is everyone's friend.

I still feel that if a gay university-student wishes to sleep with a gay teacher it is no one else's business. Also, all teachers are open to seduction by seductive students of any age: something the law cannot deal with. Political correctness based on American Puritanism does not apply here. Otherwise, Plato would have been jailed! Teachers are human and vulnerable. Child sexuality is still not understood well enough.

The same Saibaba had a friend whose gay father fellated him. The mother, having read the son's diary then demanded sex from him too. The boy fled to medical school.

Most students are helpful. Kathy Malone showed her *Mother Hoshang* (on me) at the MoMA, N.Y.

IV

My dad had to die someday.

All Bombay called sister in America to announce the death but would not phone me in India. Sister called a friend of mine to announce the news to me and he called me.

What are you going to do?

Nothing, I said.

I did not shed a single tear.

I did not have money to fly to the funeral (to be held within seven hours of death, according to Parsi custom). I did not wish to see my Bombay sister who had ordered me out of our house, nor the hordes of stepmother's beggarly relatives. (It turned out she had fourteen half-brothers and sisters by three fathers, all of whom predeceased the mother.)

My father's body was picked clean by vultures within minutes. (So was his wealth, five and a half crores of it, by stepmother's relatives.) Having no rituals to deal with grief I visited the Dalai Lama who blessed me. (At mother's death I grieved for three years.)

My friend Yunus had a dream of a death within my family. He insisted we visit Bombay. I was reluctant to go to my father and we slept away half the next day in the cheap Parsi hotel at Grant Road, where I am forced to stay when in Bombay.

I dreamed a black stallion ran full tilt at me. I rolled over onto the side of the dirt road to avoid being hit. Instead of hitting me the horsed stopped where I had stood and backtracked.

I knew Dad's death would leave me unharmed.

After phoning both his office and home to no avail, we decided to return to Hyderabad when I saw my father, blind and limping, running towards his car at Bombay's Victoria Terminus, before a cop ticketed him. I ran after him and cried: Daddy!

Who are you?

Your child! I said.

Which one? he asked. (My voice resembles sister's and he was partially blind.) He took me by hand, away from the traffic, to the side of the road and began observing sadly my eyes and my smile, my mother's!

Cut your hair! You look like Rip Van Winkle.

His last words to me. A week later he died. I had met my father in a city of forty million souls, by accident, a week before his death.

Six months later I visited stepmother. 'How sweet!' exclaims the witch in the story. Father had had a heart attack six months earlier. I was not informed. He had called me at office asking me to resign my teaching job. I had refused.

His wife gave me my half of the studio photo I had taken with dad at college graduation; dad's half she kept!

I left wordlessly.

He had earlier come to Hyderabad to bribe me with money (my inheritance). I turned down his offer. He asked to see my lodgings: an attic room newly built, rented at Rs 700 monthly. A mattress on the floor with a handloom bed sheet given by Laxma Goud, a pot of water, a Walkman (bought from my severance pay at Pune), a valise of clothes, my textbooks. He later made much mockery of my poverty. My sister encouraged him in this. (She still repeats the story to me at every American visit of mine.) Actually, he was embittered that his only son could not be bought in a lifetime of buying people.

I could not weep for six months. I was on sabbatical and dumbly watched the TV all day as a cat does its reflection in a mirror. At a midnight rerun of Raj Kapoor's *Aawara* (1953), which for me epitomizes my parents' ill-fated romance, the dam burst. I wept for a full hour. And then wept no more.

Yunus died two years later, at twenty-seven, under the wheels of a bus. He was inebriated. Our love has been catalogued in my four books of poems for him. His father was emotionally illiterate though his teacher mother was kind to me. He drank all of us out of hearth and home: an uneducated, unprincipled manipulator, a drug addict and a whoremonger. The government hospital eviscerated his body of all internal organs and sent the body home after four days. His mother turned mad at the sight. The body had stitches from belly to throat, a dark bloody bruise on the left side of the head on which he had fallen from his bike. He looked as if he was asleep, I was told. I was in South Africa, returning from a very squally safari on a dark night. 'Someone will die tonight!' I had told myself in the skidding tourist taxi. It was Yunus, the love of my life, who was fated to die that day. (Like Siva he could continue the sex act even after being spent. He was everyone's sex target.) His father drank himself to death four years later.

Siva's dance of death: He wears skulls and a moon in his hair. He dances at new moon in a graveyard which is the barren and bereft heart of his lovers. With each turning he births night and light, a new aeon.

My sister called me to say she was dying of emphysema. Death's long list:

Mother

Father

Yunus

My teachers. Virgil Lokke/Mr Bache (my Shakespeare teacher), Anaïs Nin

now, Sister...

Everyone I ever loved, dead. Those who do not love me, thriving! Life's supreme trick on us.

Sister has been a long time dying, thirteen years on an

oxygen machine. Her lungs turned into scar tissue by three tuberculosis attacks: each time one-third of the lung goes. Now her left lung is colonised by an airborne spore. She cannot beat it as she is allergic to penicillin. (Father over-medicated us in childhood). Her first childhood attack was in boarding school, infected by an old woman caretaker. My mother, then pregnant with middle sister, dreamed a child's coffin was carried by nuns to the Panchgani graveyard. Father refused to bring home our sister. Mother braved a mountain journey by state transport bus and brought her home. The second attack occurred in Chicago, washing shop windows on Michigan Avenue in the snow to get even with father who refused to recognise her first 'marriage' (actually a long-lasting live-in relationship) and who cut off funds. To repay a Chicago University scholarship she drove forty miles each way in winter to paraplegics she taught. She was found to be allergic to thirty-six out of a possible forty-two substances! Indiana Steel Mills, Gary, belched smoke into her beautiful lakeside home at four each afternoon. On my visits to her my eyes would smart and we would huddle in her air-conditioned bedroom. My sister had a business renovating ghetto homes she bought cheap, renting them out until the resale price was profitable. Both the men in her life helped her out with manual labour in her business. She herself used to strip paint off old walls, inhaling lethal fumes of industrial-strength paint-strippers. The final attack occurred when her second love left her for a twenty-year-old Chinese student, a sixty-year-old professor. A late romance with a young Mexican gardener also soured. She lay exhausted and bedridden, a millionaire.

As a response to Death, I foreswore everything dear to me:

My books, left at sister's in America (400 of them) I asked her to donate to the Black Chicago Junior College she taught at.

Likewise, my 400 Western classical records were sold $1 apiece at her garage sales. I foreswore luxuries: no big home, servants, car or expensive holidays.

My books I give away now to people after reading them.

My old clothes I give to indigent boys. My own clothes are gifted to me. I do not shop. Anaïs Nin's letters to me I gifted to Hyderabad's American Library.

My letters to sister, preserved by her, I gave away to Michael Feini, an ex-student and my future editor.

I foreswore love. Sex, I still have in plenty. Sex is what makes me feel completely alive.

When stepmother called me I told her:

You are no one to me. Please do not call. Next time, I will insult you. I cannot even spend all I earn. I certainly do not want anything from my father.

And I disconnected the call. She repeated my words before a Judge and, to prejudice him told him, I was gay. The Judge let her keep all the gifts my father gave her but she had to share with us all the property in father's sole possession at his death.

Sister in Bombay dragged her to court for ten years, and now sister is almost penniless. I had written twenty books in twenty years. I had made pain into poetry. The dream of Dad's death not harming me came true. I signed over everything to sister in India.

At sixty I wrote the 266-page *Forbidden Sex/Text* for Routledge, London.

Ardhanareeshwara is nothing but a combination of Shiva and Vishnu. An avatar is an ardhanareeshwara. I am both male and female. The combination of Shiva and Vishnu together is the Dakshinamurthy roopam (form).

The avatar lies in the middle because He or She must know you both from the outside (mind) and the inside (body). I am feminine inside and masculine outside. I can understand and communicate with the male and female only when I am distanced from both and beyond both.

After forty years of writing I was invited to read at Bombay's National Centre for the Performing Arts (run on the lines of the one in New York). Bombay's poets, some of them closet gays, did not show up. But my high school English teacher, old, blind, toothless and widowed showed up to dub me 'romantic' and 'sentimental' as usual. (She changed the last epithet to 'sensitive' and took me to the very British Bombay Gymkhana for dinner.) So did my college classmate whom I had not seen for forty years and who introduced me in the absence of anyone else: 'Even in college Hoshang had a following,' she said. That was news to me. So did the sister of another classmate who informed me my friend, her sister, had died ten years earlier of cancer, and who asked intelligent questions. So did the critic Homi Bhabha's mother, who declared herself to be eighty-two and me to be 'charming'. The sound system was perfect, the intimate room filled to capacity and the help kindly put in half an hour overtime as the reading went beyond its stipulated hour. A student of mine sat beside my teacher: So forty years were nicely spanned in forty minutes. What do they call my poetry? Postcolonial and postmodern. Or, World Poetry or New Age Poetry (a name I like best). I had come home.

Placid came back into my life: on crutches! I wept to see him thus. A life of overindulgence had led to this. He had built the Kalpakam nuclear power plant for India. We had set a Christmas date for our rebonding. I spent the vacation writing my love nostalgia (in *Bombay My Bombay!*). He was the handsomest man I ever knew. He died at sixty-five of complications from a heart surgery.

The final holocaust: of fame. Posthumous fame has been predicted for me. *Yaraana* made me a celebrity: reviews, interviews, speaking invitations, book launches, documentary films on me. I went along for a while. *Deccan Chronicle* made me into a page-3 person. Horrors! I have thrown out my TV, disconnected my phone. I do not own a cell phone. I do not answer the doorbell. Few, who know it, reach me at my email address. I do not care for publicity. I visit sister yearly in America. I love the few friends I have. Erotic love was not in my fate.

When Laura Riding, poet, had uninvited visitors she would yell out of an upstairs window: 'I am not in.'

Anaïs Nin too does not live here anymore.

Nor does 'Hoshang Merchant'.